THE KAYAK SHOP

THE KAYAK SHOP

Three Elegant Wooden Kayaks Anyone Can Build

Chris Kulczycki

Ragged Mountain Press
Camden, Maine

Published by Ragged Mountain Press, a division of McGraw-Hill, Inc.

10 9 8 7 6 5

Library of Congress Cataloging-in-Publication Data

Kulczycki, Chris, 1958–
The kayak shop : three elegant wooden kayaks anyone can build / Chris Kulczycki.
p. cm.
Includes index.
ISBN 0-87742-367-9 (acid-free paper)
1. Kayaks—Design and construction—Amateurs's manuals. I. Title.
VM353.K85 1993
623.8'29—dc20 93–23886
CIP

Questions regarding the content of this book should be addressed to:
Ragged Mountain Press
P.O. Box 220
Camden, ME 04843

Questions regarding the ordering of this book should be addressed to:
McGraw-Hill, Inc.
Customer Service Department
P.O. Box 547
Blacklick, OH 43004
Retail Customers: 1-800-822-8158
Bookstores: 1-800-722-4726

A portion of the profits from the sale of each Ragged Mountain Press book is donated to an environmental cause.

This book is printed on 60-pound Renew Opaque Vellum, an acid-free paper which contains 50 percent recycled waste paper (preconsumer) and 10 percent postconsumer waste paper.

Printed by R. R. Donnelley, Crawfordsville, IN
Design by Silverline Studio, Camden, Maine
Production by Janet Robbins
Edited by Jim Babb, Michael S. Crowley, and Pamela Benner

For Annette

"For she is such a smart little craft,
Such a neat little, sweet little craft–
Such a bright little,
Tight little,
Slight little,
Light little,
Trim little, slim little craft."

—W. S. Gilbert, *Ruddigore II*

Contents

Chapter 1
The Wooden Kayak

This book will guide you through building a round-bottomed, high-performance 16-foot single-seat kayak; a hard-chine 18-foot sea kayak; and a compounded-plywood 20-foot double. Plans for each of these three boats are reproduced and discussed in Chapter 5. But the same methods used to build these kayaks can be applied to building many other kayaks drawn by other designers or by you.

I'll assume that you have just an elementary knowledge of woodworking; those of you who are expert boatbuilders or cabinetmakers will have to bear with us. And I'll also assume that you know a little about kayaks—that is, that you've paddled a few.

The themes here are simplicity, light weight, economy, and aesthetics. While some designs require that you construct large jigs and strongbacks to build the kayak on, the designs discussed here don't, nor do they rely on extensive frameworks. You won't need to buy any unusual tools, and the materials you'll use, while not available everywhere, can certainly be ordered and shipped anywhere. These kayaks are at least a third lighter than most plastic kayaks, yet they are rigid and strong. They can be built for a half or even a quarter the

This hard-chine sea kayak, the *Queen Charlotte,* is one of several seakindly and popular boats sold in kit form by the Pygmy Boat Company. Its designer, John Lockwood, is a pioneer in computerized hull development. (Photo courtesy Pygmy Boat Company)

The Pocomoke and the Yare, two designs featured in this book, are good examples of the complex shapes possible with compounded-plywood designs. The Pocomoke is 19 feet, 10 inches long and weighs 52 pounds; the 16-foot 3-inch Yare weighs 26 pounds.

cost of a comparable fiberglass kayak, but they often perform better. And they are, at least to my eye, quite handsome.

Why Wood?

A tree must bend and flex thousands of times each windy day, millions of times in a year, yet it still returns to its original shape. Its branches must be strong and light, yet stiff enough to hold their load of leaves. Protected by its coating of bark, it must resist the assaults of sun, water, and wind. These same characteristics—light weight, strength, resistance to fatigue, and durability—make wood an excellent material for the construction of your kayak.

Plywood kayaks are light. That's me holding up my 26-pound Yare. This is the way I usually carry it to the water. (Photo by Annette Najjar)

Though wood has lower initial strength than some other materials used in boatbuilding, its other properties make up for this. Consider that even with the arrival of such exotic materials as carbon fiber, Nomex, and Kevlar, some of today's fastest multihull sailboats are built of wood and epoxy. There are few craft that experience the loads and the stresses of an ocean-racing multihull and that pay so high a price in performance for extra weight.

Beyond weight and strength, stiffness and resistance to fatigue must be considered when selecting the material for a kayak. Studies have shown wood to be up to 10 times stiffer than fiberglass by weight, and nearly 6 times stiffer than Kevlar/epoxy composite. Though these studies aren't directly applicable to kayak construction, they do illustrate that wood is a very stiff material and a stiff boat tends to be faster, particularly in calm water, since energy is not wasted in flexing the hull.

A kayak must have more than just initial strength; its strength must be retained despite repeated cycles of tension and compression from rough seas and spirited paddling. Wood loses very little strength even after millions of cycles of loading and unloading. That tree, flexing millions of times a year, may live for hundreds or even thousands of years if man or natural disaster doesn't intervene. This resistance to fatigue gives wood an advantage over many materials when a long-lasting and reliable hull is the objective.

Toughness or resistance to tearing, puncturing, and abrasion is an important consideration, particularly if a kayak is launched from and landed on rocky shores. Fiberglass and polyethylene have some advantage over wood in this quality, but by sheathing the wooden hull with a thin layer of fiberglass cloth, Kevlar, or Dynel its toughness can be greatly improved.

Woods's traditional drawbacks have largely been solved by modern technology. The problem of rot has been greatly reduced, though not totally eliminated, by modern epoxy saturation methods. The problem of finding suitable wood has been solved by the advent of truly high-quality plywoods. And the problem of waterproof glue has been eliminated by modern epoxy systems. Modern methods of wooden-boat building bear little resemblance to those of 50 years ago. Wood has become a high-tech material.

However much we appreciate the engineering properties of wood, it is wood's aesthetic qualities that are most remarkable. No other material inspires such a bond between the paddler and the kayak. People seem drawn to wooden boats, perhaps as a reaction to the profusion of artificial materials that surround us. Wooden kayaks feel better and paddle better than do fiberglass boats. I don't know why this is; perhaps I only imagine it—but a lot of other folks imagine it,

The Cape Charles is another hard-chine sea kayak design, and the third boat described in this book. It's 18 feet long and weighs about 40 pounds.

professional boatbuilders. I can even borrow a tool I need from some of the other members.

The hardest part of building your own kayak is getting started. By opening this book you've done that. But before you take saw to wood, read the entire book. Knowing what comes next can save you substantial time and trouble when you're building.

If you don't have much time, you can buy a kayak kit. This Chesapeake Light Craft kit becomes a Yare.

Chapter 2
The Design

Kayaks are among the simplest of boats, yet thousands of kayak designs have been created, each of them someone's idea of the perfect boat. Your first step in building a kayak is choosing a design or drawing your own. If you're an experienced kayaker, you'll probably have an idea of how a boat will paddle just from looking at it. If you're not experienced, take every opportunity to paddle different boats before selecting one to build. In either case, knowing a little about how kayak, paddler, and water interact and about the elements of a kayak's design will help you make a wise choice.

Kayak design is not a science; it's a blend of art, intuition, and engineering. This becomes obvious to me every time I launch a new design. Whether I've drawn the boat or built it to someone else's design, I am always surprised by some aspect of the kayak's performance. Still, using a blend of experience and theory, you'll have a pretty good shot at choosing the boat that's right for you.

Length

Length is usually the first dimension you'll look at. To a large degree, a kayak's length determines how fast it can go, how stable it is, and

Paddle as many boats as you can and see how far you can push them. Clay Corry tries out my prototype Skua 16.

how much it will hold. There are really two separate lengths that must be considered for every boat. The first is the length overall, or *LOA*: this is the distance between the outside faces of the bow and stern. The length on the waterline, or *LWL*, is the more important length measurement: the LWL is the distance between the *immersed* ends of the kayak when it's normally loaded.

Most benefits of length are due to a long LWL, and not to a long LOA. A boat with a LOA much longer than its LWL is said to have long overhangs. Long overhanging bows and sterns are often added to a design for cosmetic reasons. Some paddlers feel that long overhanging bows are beneficial in rough waters. But similar advantages can be achieved with a moderate overhang by increasing the volume in the bow. Long overhangs, particularly if they are upswept as in some "Greenland-style" kayaks, add considerable lateral surface area that makes a boat more difficult to handle in strong winds.

Most paddlers know that a boat's top speed is related to its length. A boat creates a bow wave where it cuts through the water and a stern wave as the water comes together again at the boat's end; in order for waves to move faster they must be farther apart. So a long boat, with its bow and stern waves farther apart, will be able to go faster. A boat's theoretical top speed, or *hull speed*, in knots (a knot is 1.15 m.p.h.) is 1.34 times the square root of the LWL. Now before you write to ask me why Uncle Fred's 17-foot speedboat can go 50 knots while your 17-foot sea kayak will only go 5 knots, let me explain that this rule doesn't apply to high-powered planing boats, which slide over the water, not through it. Actually, your kayak can also attain very high speeds when surfing down waves. Even on flat water, a kayak, like many boats with very narrow hulls, is capable of speeds slightly higher than its theoretical hull speed.

The importance of length as related to speed can be overemphasized. A paddler can generate about one-quarter horsepower, so the limiting factor in speed is the drag that your paddling must overcome and not theoretical hull speed. Once the kayak's LWL approaches 17 feet or so, little or no speed will be gained by lengthening it. You'll rarely paddle fast enough to achieve hull speed in a kayak. At average touring speeds, however, a boat with a longer LWL will be easier to paddle, assuming everything else is equal.

There's more to be gained from length than just speed. If you compare two kayaks of different lengths but otherwise similar design, you'll find that the longer boat has several advantages over the shorter one. The longer boat won't pitch as violently in steep waves, and it will be more stable. It will have a higher volume and will hold more gear. And the longer boat will track, or go in a straight line, better than the shorter kayak.

On the other hand, there are some disadvantages to longer kayaks. Comparing the same two boats, you'll notice that the longer one is less maneuverable, requires more materials to build, and is heavier and more expensive. Finally, a long boat will be harder to store and transport. Single sea kayaks with a LWL of 14 feet to 18 feet seem ideal. Doubles appear to work best with a LWL of 17 feet to 20 feet. Flat-water kayaks, very wide kayaks, and kayaks intended for lighter loads may be shorter. High-performance kayaks and racing kayaks, if not limited by rules, may be longer.

Beam and Cross Section

After length, you'll look at a kayak's beam, or width. Beam, like length, affects a kayak's volume, stability, and speed. You must consider the beam both at the waterline and overall. Closely related to beam is the cross-sectional shape of the kayak's hull. It may be round-bottomed, flat-bottomed, V-bottomed, or, more commonly, a combination of these shapes.

It's generally thought that wider boats are more stable. This is often, though not always, true. Stability has two elements: initial and ultimate. *Initial stability* is seen in a skiff or a beamy, flat-bottomed kayak. A boat with high initial stability doesn't feel tippy, or tender, but if it's heeled over too far it capsizes without warning. A boat with high *ultimate stability*, such as a kayak with a rounded bottom and flared sides, may be tender at first but as it heels, more of the hull is immersed, increasing resistance to capsize. Initial heeling actually helps skilled paddlers control the boat by enabling them to easily lean into a turn and into waves when in rough seas. Round-bottomed and V-bottomed boats and craft with very narrow waterline beams usually have lower initial stability. Boats with flared sides and high volume tend to have high ultimate stability.

A good way to improve stability is not by increasing the beam but by lowering the boat's center of gravity. Moving a kayak's seat down an inch or two can result in a dramatic increase in stability. All the weight in a kayak should be placed as low as possible, including your seat.

Shorter kayaks must be wider so they are able to hold their intended cargos. But there are several disadvantages to beamy kayaks. They are usually slower than narrower boats and often don't track as well. In addition, a normal-length paddle may strike the gunnels of a wide kayak, and beamy kayaks can be unattractive. For single-seat kayaks, a beam of 19 inches to 26 inches is reasonable while doubles may be as wide as 32 inches.

Prismatic Coefficient and Hull Form

Another measurement related to a boat's beam and cross section is its *prismatic coefficient*, or Cp. A kayak's Cp describes how full or fine ended the hull is. A boat with a high Cp has its volume distributed along its length, causing the ends to have a "full" shape. A boat with a low Cp has its volume concentrated near the center, and its ends are finely tapered. Cp is the ratio between the volume of displacement (how much water a loaded boat displaces) and the volume of a prism that has the same length as the LWL and the same cross-sectional area as the widest part of the submerged portion of the hull.

Most kayaks have a Cp between 0.45 and 0.60. Cp is important because of its relationship to hull resistance and the boat's motion. A boat with very full ends, or a high Cp, will tend to "push" its bow and stern waves farther apart and toward the ends of the hull. As you remember, the farther apart the waves are, the faster the boat is capable of moving. Of course when the Cp gets too high the waves get too big, and too much energy is required to push them; we then have a barge. A kayak with very fine ends, a low Cp, won't make efficient use of its length to achieve a high hull speed because the bow and stern waves will be too close together; however, such a boat may be very efficient at low and medium speeds. Most designers don't actually calculate a kayak's Cp; instead, they rely on experience and a good eye to draw the proper balance of fullness and fineness in the ends.

A kayak's bow and stern must also have enough buoyancy to stay above water. When boats with low Cp's are paddled in steep seas, the ends tend to dig into the faces of the waves. This can cause broaching when paddling downwind and make the boat difficult to control in other circumstances. With fine-ended designs, the hull should flare above the waterline to increase the kayak's reserve buoyancy.

The designer must also decide where to place the boat's maximum beam. If the widest part is at or near the midpoint of the boat's length, the kayak is said to have a *symmetrical form*. When the maximum beam is forward of the midpoint, the boat has a *fish-form* hull; if it is aft of center, the boat has a *swede-form* hull.

It's thought that the fish-form and symmetrical hulls are more efficient than swede-form designs, but the difference, if any, is slight. You've probably noticed that many modern kayaks appear to be swede-form. Because a boat's bow overhang is usually much longer than its stern overhang, the maximum waterline beam of a symmetrical-form boat may be aft of the center of its overall length, causing it to appear to be a swede-form. Some designers prefer to place the maximum beam aft of the cockpit so that the paddle will more easily clear the deck. Also, many paddlers prefer the appearance of a swede-form boat; perhaps this is a reaction to the shape of some racing kayaks that are built to specific measurement rules, giving them the swede-form.

Wetted-Surface Area

The *wetted-surface area* is the area of the hull below the waterline. At low speeds, the friction of the hull's skin is a greater source of resistance to forward progress than the waves formed by the kayak's forward motion. So a long, narrow boat with a high theoretical hull speed but a large wetted surface requires more energy to paddle at low speed than a short, fat boat with a minimal wetted surface. Paddlers sometimes buy long kayaks thinking they'll be able to go faster; for short bursts they will, but at normal touring speeds they may actually end up moving slower than in a shorter boat with less wetted-surface area.

The kayak on the left has less initial stability and less volume than the boat on the right; however, the kayak on the right also has a larger wetted-surface area.

Boats with a very low wetted-surface area have cross sections resembling a semicircle; these hulls have very low initial stability. In extreme cases, such as flat-water racing kayaks, they can only be handled by expert paddlers. Touring-kayak hulls have flatter cross sections to increase initial stability, which adds wetted-surface area. Hard-chine and flat-bottomed boats have higher wetted-surface areas; however, they also tend to have larger load-carrying capacities—and that may be more important on long trips.

Volume

A kayak's volume is sometimes expressed in gallons or in cubic feet, but more often as high, medium, or low. Volume is influenced by a kayak's length, beam, prismatic coefficient, and depth or deck height. A high-volume kayak is one that holds tons of gear and a big paddler. For long-distance touring, you'll need to have sufficient volume to pack camping gear and supplies. A high-volume boat is usually slower and heavier than one with low or medium volume, but it is also drier and more comfortable. In strong winds, a high-volume kayak, with more freeboard, will be more difficult to control than a boat with a lower profile and lower volume.

Physical size is also important in choosing your kayak's volume. If you have a small build, you may feel uncomfortable or "lost" in a high-volume boat. You may also lack the weight to effectively lean such a boat. Larger paddlers often feel cramped in low-volume kayaks. Unless you plan extended trips or are particularly heavy or tall, there's little reason to choose a very high-volume kayak.

Rocker and Rudders

Rocker is the upward curve of the kayak's keel line over its length. If you place a kayak with pronounced rocker, such as a whitewater kayak, on a flat floor, the middle of the keel will touch the floor while the ends (at the waterline) will be several inches above the floor. Such a boat will turn easily but be difficult to paddle in a straight line. If a boat without any rocker is placed on the same floor, it will touch the floor over most of its length. This kayak will be difficult to turn but easy to paddle straight.

Tracking is more important than turning ability in touring and sea kayaks. To strike a balance between tracking and turning, most sea kayaks are designed with a small amount of rocker—one to three inches. Longer boats, boats with V-shaped hulls, or with very fine ends can have more rocker without compromising tracking. Also, a kayak with rocker is easier to maneuver in rough water. It's a common misconception that adding rocker makes a boat slower: actually, modern flat-water racing kayaks often have considerable rocker.

In heavy winds and seas, rudders are invaluable. They are also useful in doubles and in heavily loaded singles. Any kayak that must rely on a rudder to be handled properly, however, is unsafe. Rudders and skegs shouldn't be used as a remedy for poorly designed hulls. A boat that's deficient in tracking or turning can have a rudder added, but why not design it properly in the first place? A movable skeg can also be used to balance a boat in rough conditions, as illustrated by Frank Goodman's fine designs, and a skeg is far simpler to design and install. Rudders can and do fail, so they should be considered a convenience, not an essential.

Deck and Cockpit

The deck is an integral part of a kayak's design. It adds enormous rigidity and strength to the hull. A deck must have sufficient *camber*, or curvature, to accommodate the paddlers knees, feet, and gear. Camber increases a kayak's volume and allows the deck to quickly shed water and keep the paddler drier. A kayak with a cambered or peaked deck is easier to Eskimo roll. Decks that are too high, however, increase windage and make the boat more difficult to handle in extreme weather conditions.

Many plywood kayak decks are composed of flat, as opposed to cambered, sections. Such decks often have a tendency to flex or "oil-can." Most are designed with the mistaken belief that they are easier to build than curved decks. In fact, cambered decks are often simpler to construct and are usually lighter and stronger.

A kayak's cockpit must fit the paddler; it must be both snug and comfortable. Cockpits and seats can be customized with closed-cell foam padding, such as Ethafoam. The cockpit opening should allow the paddler to enter and exit the boat quickly and efficiently, though it must not be so wide or long that the paddler's knees can't be braced under the deck.

A sea kayak's coaming must be strong enough and low enough to sit on when performing a wet reentry. However, if the kayak is to be used primarily in calm water and without a spray skirt, then the coaming may be higher to help keep the paddler dry. In this case, the coaming doesn't have to be so heavily built because wet reentries are rare in calm-water paddling.

Choosing a Design

As you consider an existing design or draw your own, remember that any design is a compromise. It's relatively easy to design a boat that's well suited to one specific purpose—a very fast boat, for example, or one that's capable of carrying heavy loads. But designing a boat that can do several things well, that's an art.

By comparing a new design to kayaks you've paddled, you can get a fair idea of how it will suit you. But don't get hung up on "numbers"—you'll never notice an extra inch or two of length or a ¼ inch more rocker. If the design is 90 percent right, build it and go paddling.

All else aside, I've found that prettier boats are better boats. If you look at a new design and it doesn't move you, if it isn't a kayak that'll bring a smile to your face whenever you see it sitting on the beach, then it isn't the boat for you.

Plans

One of the great pleasures of boatbuilding is deciding which boat to build. You can spend many happy hours looking through back issues of *WoodenBoat* magazine, *Boatbuilding, messing about in Boats*, old issues of *Small Boat Journal* (sadly *Small Boat Journal* is all powerboats now, and its name has changed), and other magazines, looking at various kayak designs and advertisements for plans. But sooner or later it's time to send off a check and unroll your plans. If you're new to boatbuilding, the plans may seem complicated and confusing. But most boat plans are drawn in a similar style. Once you get the hang of reading one set of plans, you'll be able read most others as easily as you're reading this book.

Reading Plans

Traditionally, a set of plans for a small boat offers three views. There is a *profile view* showing the boat from the side; a *half-breadth*, or *plan, view* displaying the boat from the top; and a *body plan*, or *sections*, showing a combination front and back view. A set of lines resembling and serving the same purpose as contour lines on a map may be superimposed over these views; these are descriptively called the boat's lines. Boatbuilders measure and scale up these lines to full size using a process called *lofting*. Many designers also include a table of measurements from the centerline to the edge of the hull at particular cross sections. These are called *stations*, and the table is called the *table of offsets*. Offsets make the job of lofting far easier and faster.

Now if all this has you considering taking up bowling instead of kayak building, I have some good news. Most kayak plans drawn for amateur builders contain measurements for all the parts and don't require lofting or using tables of offsets. In many plan sets there are even full-size patterns for parts such as seats, footbraces, bulkheads, and coamings. Still, before you start building, it's important to study the boat's lines to know how the hull will be shaped.

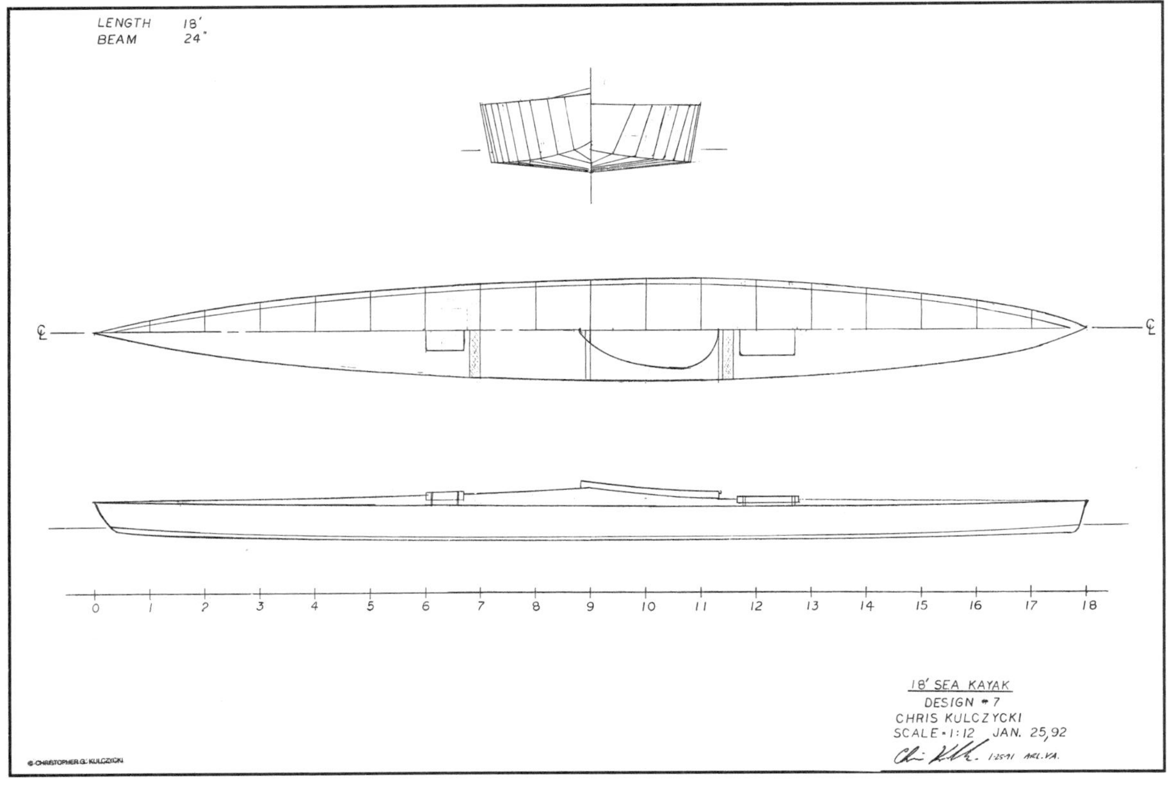

This preliminary plan of a sea kayak consists of a body plan (top), a deck plan (middle), and a profile (bottom).

In addition to the main views of the boat, there will also be a few expanded views in the plans. Like close-ups, these show additional details. They are usually self-explanatory but are critical to understanding how the boat goes together. There will usually be sketches of the seat, hatches, footbraces, and other little parts that would only crowd the main drawing if they were detailed on the primary views.

In addition to the plan sheets, you'll need the *scantlings* and/or the bill of materials. The scantlings tell what material each part is made of, and the bill of materials tells you what will be needed. On kayak plans, both lists may be combined or the scantlings may be incorporated into the building directions. Study the bill of materials carefully so you can estimate that other important bill: your bill *for* materials.

Reproduced in Chapter 5 are the plans for three kayaks. These plans, like most published in books and magazines, are reduced from full size to fit on these pages; thus, they lose some clarity and detail. When you decide to build a particular kayak, you should invest in a full-size set of plans from the designer. It's certainly possible to build boats from plans reproduced in books and magazines, but having the full-size set and accompanying instructions will save you many hours and doubts, especially if you are a novice builder. The few extra dollars you spend will be forgotten when the boat is finished.

Modifying Plans

All paddlers have their own ideas of the perfect boat. One of the great advantages of building a boat is that your personal wants and needs can be accommodated. Modifications, if they are well thought out, will make the boat ideally suited to your paddling style. But before deciding on a design change, consider that a boat's designer has put substantial thought and experience into his design, so you should think carefully about any changes. Will they affect the strength of the kayak? Will it still be as seaworthy? If you put in a larger cockpit, for example, will the boat have less rigidity? Can you find a spray skirt to fit the cockpit? You may want a stronger boat and decide to increase the thickness of the hull skin, but the thicker wood might not conform to the desired shape. A better solution might be to add a layer of fiberglass cloth over the bottom. If the changes you want to make seem major or you're unsure of the effect they'll have on the boat's strength, then write to the designer for advice.

Designing Your Own Kayak

Many experienced paddlers are capable of designing their own kayaks, if they are willing to devote a fair amount of time and study to the task. If you choose to try your own design, consider starting with an existing design that you like and slowly redrawing it to meet your needs. Designing from a "blank sheet of paper" is much more difficult, and I wouldn't recommend trying it until you've built a few boats.

Scale Models

So you've designed the perfect kayak or found the perfect design, but you wish you could see a three-dimensional representation before you devote all that time to building it. Scale models have been used by designer's for almost as long as boats have been built. In fact, a traditional way to design a boat is to carve half the hull to scale (a half-model or half-hull) and to take measurements from it when drawing the boat's lines. Since you will be building plywood kayaks, it's only logical that you make plywood models.

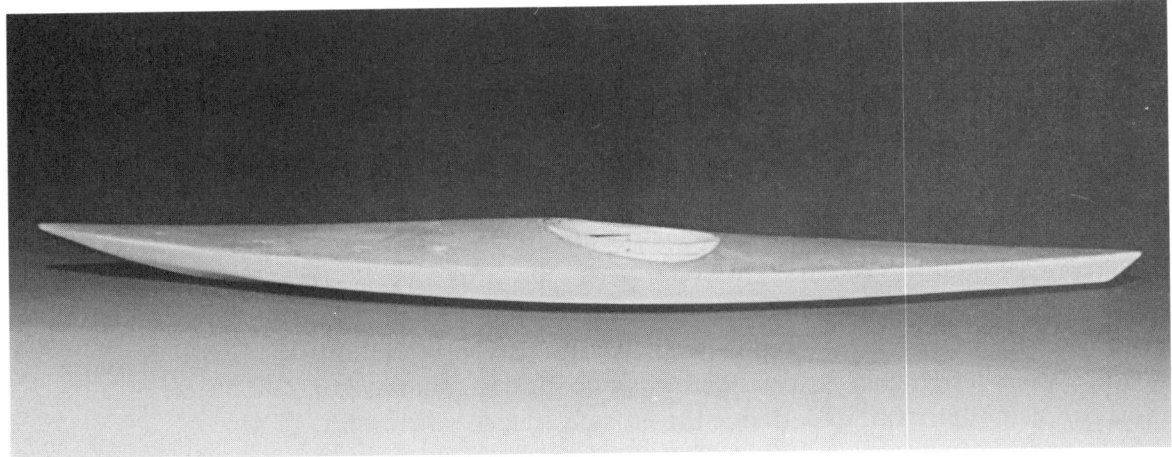

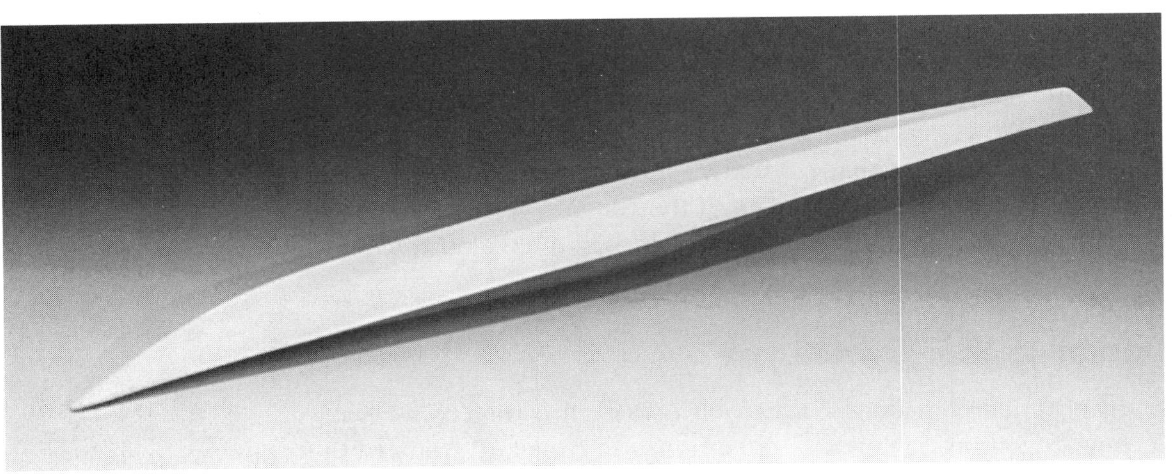

Boatbuilder and photographer Bob Grove built this handsome model of a sea kayak he was considering building.

The plywood to use is $\frac{1}{32}$-inch or .8mm aircraft-grade birch. At a scale of one inch to one foot (a model of a 16-foot kayak is 16 inches long) the $\frac{1}{32}$-inch plywood bends to about the same degree as 3mm or 4mm plywood does on a full-size boat.

Before you start building, check all your measuring tools against each other. It's not uncommon to find a tape that doesn't agree exactly with a yardstick. I make all critical distance measurements with my tapemeasure or my metal 12-inch rule. I am certain that these are correct, so if there's any error I know who to blame.

The tool used more than any other will be your tapemeasure; Stanley and Lufkin make the best ones. The most durable and easiest to use are the 25-foot models with 1-inch-wide blades. The 30-foot x 1-inch tapes are also good, but their springs wear out sooner. Short, thin tapemeasures are best left for hanging pictures and building birdhouses.

I use a 12-inch metal rule divided into $\frac{1}{64}$-inch marks for measuring critical thicknesses like scarf lines, fastener lengths, drill-bit diameters, and other small dimensions. I also have a set of vernier calipers for critical measuring, but I'll admit that they're really overkill. You'll need a long rule to use as a straightedge; I use an inexpensive 36-inch steel drafting rule. For laying out longer lines, a piece of thin string or carpenter's chalkline is fine.

More measuring tools: a carpenter's square, a try square, and a nonessential vernier caliper.

In addition to tools for measuring distances, you'll need tools for measuring angles. A carpenter's square is needed to ensure right angles when you lay out the kayak's hull and deck panels. If you don't already have one, buy the large 24- x 18-inch version. A small 6-inch or 9-inch try square is handy for laying out and checking right angles in close quarters. The traditional boatbuilder's adjustable square, or bevel square, is also very useful—I wouldn't be without one. If you need to lay out radii, you can use a piece of string, but a set of trammels, which acts like a bar compass, makes the job easier. One last measuring device you'll want is a protractor; this can be a cheap, plastic student model, though larger versions are easier to read.

Once you've made a measurement, you'll need to mark it. Some craftsmen use only a knife or a scribe because they leave thinner lines than a pencil does. Actually, I prefer to use a sharp pencil as the line is easier to see. A mechanical pencil is wonderful because it never needs sharpening, but I'm always losing mine. A useful, though not essential, tool is a marking gauge. I use it to mark scarf lines and the position of the wire holes before stitching a hull together.

Tools for Cutting

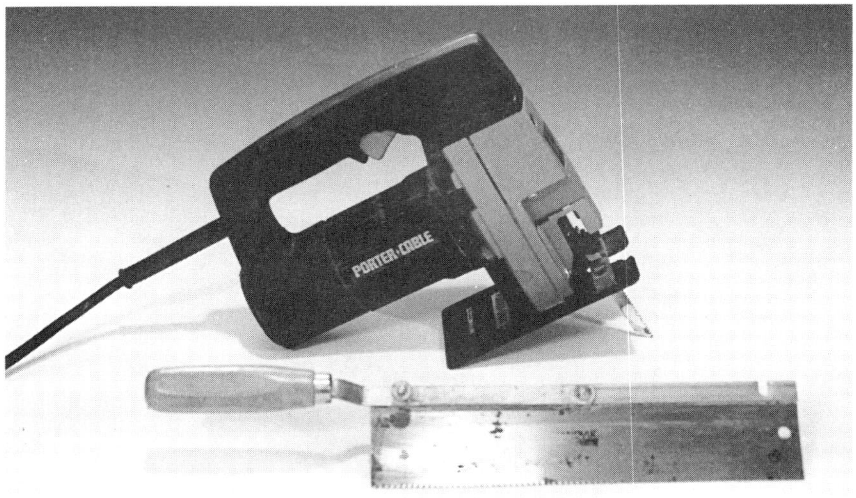

A sabersaw and a dovetail saw are essential.

The only power tool that you absolutely must have is a sabersaw. Sabersaws fall into one of two categories. There are expensive, heavy-duty professional models, and there are inexpensive, low-quality homeowner models. Though you certainly don't need the power of a professional model to cut the light materials needed for kayak building, the higher quality construction and superior blade guides on professional models make them a better choice. I use a top handle Porter Cable sabersaw that I'm quite fond of; Bosch and Hitachi also make fine sabersaws. Many boatbuilders prefer sabersaws without handles, called barrel-grip models, because they are a bit easier to control. Stay away from saws with a scroll feature; the scroll mechanism will eventually loosen, and the blade will wander and twist. Be sure any sabersaw you buy has a little blower to clear sawdust away from the blade so you can see what you're cutting. Another essential feature is a blade guide, mounted either on or just above the saw's base plate. Without this feature, the blade will tend to wander and bend as you're cutting through thick materials.

The best sabersaw blades are the bimetal type. They're often painted white, and they cost more than regular blades, but since you'll only wear out one or two blades per kayak, the additional cost is minimal. I use woodcutting blades with 10 teeth per inch.

A small handsaw is essential for accurate cuts in solid pieces. My favorite is a little Swedish dovetail saw made by Sandvik. It has a reversible, offset handle, so it can make flush cuts to either side. However, any small backsaw, tenon saw, or dovetail saw will do. Many boatbuilders and cabinetmakers are switching to a Japanese-style backsaw called a *dozuki*. They do cut incredibly fast; when my Sandvik wears out. . . .

Sooner or later you have to face the fact that some kayak parts need to be ripped from solid wood. The only tool for that job is a table saw. But unless you plan to build a lot more than one kayak, the cost of a table saw is prohibitive. Instead, arrange to use a friend's saw or pay a lumberyard to rip the sheer clamps, carlins, and other solid wood pieces. Actually, with a bit of searching, you might find the right size pieces already cut at a lumberyard.

A circular saw is useful for cutting boards to length and splitting sheets of plywood. But rather than get out my heavy old worm-drive saw, I'll often reach for a crosscut saw or a sabersaw instead. They don't cut as accurately, but most pieces will be fine-trimmed later.

Planes and Chisels

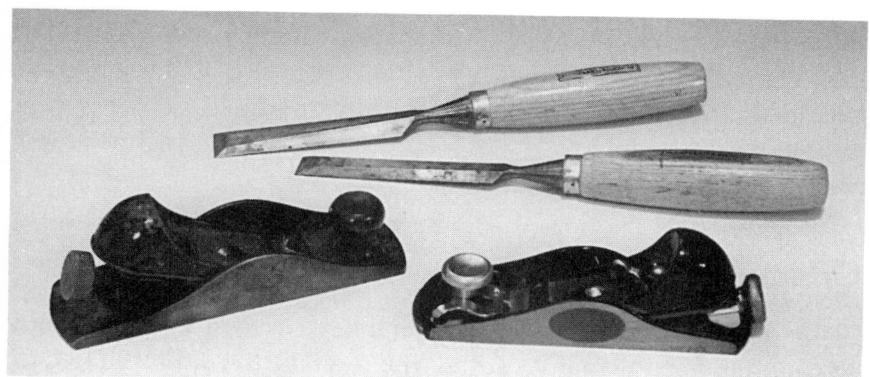

On the left is a Stanley model 220 block plane. On the right is the slightly better model 60½. A couple of chisels are also nice to have.

Woodworkers love planes, so you might be disappointed when I tell you that only a block plane is needed to build these kayaks. In fact, a block plane is likely to become your favorite tool. You'll use it to cut scarfs, to trim hull and deck panels, to clean up rough edges, and to shape small parts.

Block planes are available in standard models with an angle of about 20 degrees between the blade and the work surface and in low-angle models with an angle of 12 degrees to 13 degrees. The low-angle type is better suited to the cross-grain planing usually required in kayak building. I use a Stanley model 60½ low-angle plane; Record makes a similar plane (the Record 60½) that's a little better finished. If you already own a standard block plane, there's no need to buy a low-angle version; I used an old Stanley model 220 for years, until I dropped and cracked it.

You could certainly build a kayak without any chisels, but considering their usefulness and low cost it would be false economy. A ½-inch or ¾-inch cabinetmaker's chisel is all that you'll need. If kept very sharp, chisels can be used to trim pieces for that perfect fit. I also have a set of cheap Chinese chisels that I use for scraping glue and for other tasks that would ruin my good chisels.

Planes and chisels must be kept razor sharp to work properly. A dull plane will gouge and cause tear-outs. A dull chisel is dangerous to the boat and to the user. Buy a whetstone or water stone and use it often. If you can afford an electric water-stone sharpener, don't hesitate to get one; my little Wen electric sharpener is one of my most appreciated tools.

Staplers

Okay, this is not a traditional boatbuilder's tool. But when you need to temporarily clamp large, awkward plywood pieces, no other tool is as useful. If you fill it with stainless steel, Monel, or bronze staples, they can be left in the wood. If you think that the staples will spoil the finish, they are easy to remove and the tiny holes left behind are easy to fill. My stapler is an Arrow T-50 filled with ⅜-inch stainless steel staples.

Clamps

To build the kayaks in this book, you'll need at least 10 clamps, but 25 would not be too many. Most of them can be the old-fashioned C-clamps. Those operations that require the most clamps, gluing the cockpit coaming and the sheer clamps, can be accomplished with small 2-inch C-clamps. These can be bought from professional tool-supply companies very cheaply, so there's no excuse for running out. A few 2-inch spring clamps are also nice to have around for those times when you've only one free hand.

Light-duty bar clamps, like the popular orange Jorgensens, are the most useful large clamps. Every boatbuilder should own a couple of these in the 6-inch and 18-inch sizes. With practice they can be operated one-handed. A couple of 36-inch bar clamps or pipe clamps are handy for holding deck beams in place. Some larger C-clamps or heavy-duty 6-inch bar clamps should round out your clamp collection.

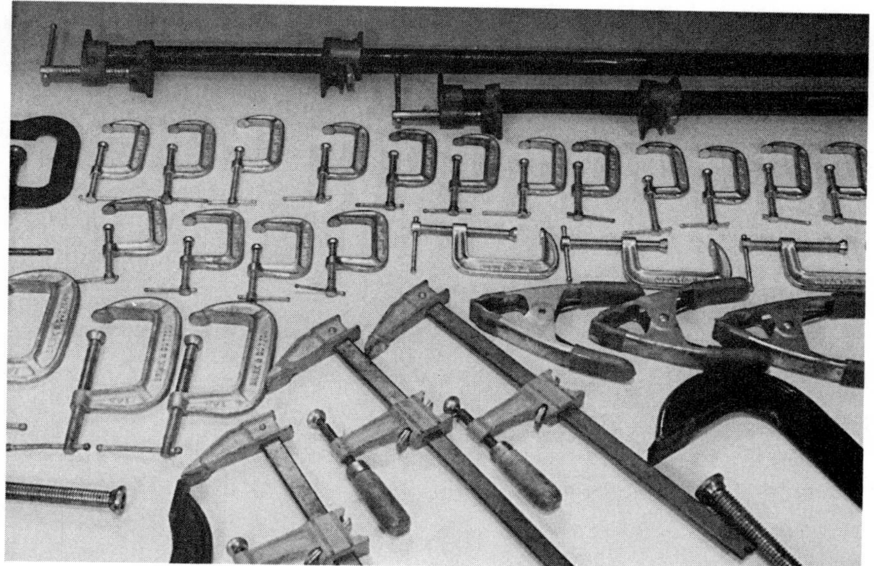

You can never have too many clamps. The little C-clamps near the top of the photo are inexpensive and most useful.

Oil or wax the clamp's threads, and they won't become fouled with epoxy. You'll often need a clamp in a hurry, so hang them all from a shelf or horizontal bar within easy reach of your work area. There are few things more frustrating than trying to untangle a pile of clamps while your carefully aligned parts slide apart.

Sanders

Sanding, like taxes, is one of the unpleasant realities of life. Compared to cold-molded or strip-planked boats, plywood kayaks

On the left is my Porter Cable random-orbital sander. It's a little faster than my reliable old Makita quarter-sheet finishing sander on the right.

don't require much sanding. You could do all that's required by hand in a few hours. Still, most of us will choose to use an electric sander.

My favorite is the quarter-sheet Makita palm sander. Many other companies make similar models, but the Makita fits my hand just right. It also sands fast enough that I can see progress, but not so fast that I accidentally sand through layers of plywood or fiberglass tape. Lately, I've been using a 5-inch random-orbital finishing sander from Porter Cable. It's a bit faster than my Makita, but it uses more expensive self-adhesive paper.

I also own a 3- x 21-inch belt sander for shaping small parts. To use it, I clamp it upside down to my workbench. If you're in a hurry, a belt sander is useful, but be forewarned that one slip and you could ruin a perfectly good kayak.

Drills

You could get by with almost any drill, including an old-fashioned eggbeater type. I use a light-duty, rechargeable Skil professional model with a built-in clutch. You don't need much drilling power to build these kayaks, so cordless drills are fine. In fact, they're almost addictive. The clutch is useful when driving screws because it prevents them from being over-driven.

You'll need a set of drill bits. Cheap drill bits bend, break, and dull quickly—they're not worth having. Instead consider a small but high-quality set of brad-point bits. Buy an extra 1⁄16-inch bit because that's the size you'll use for wire-tie holes.

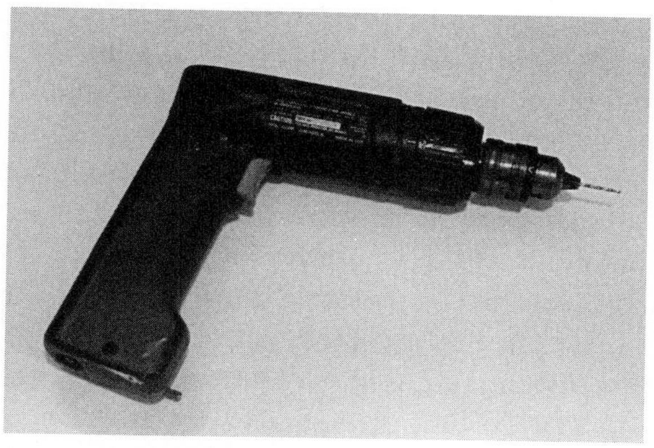

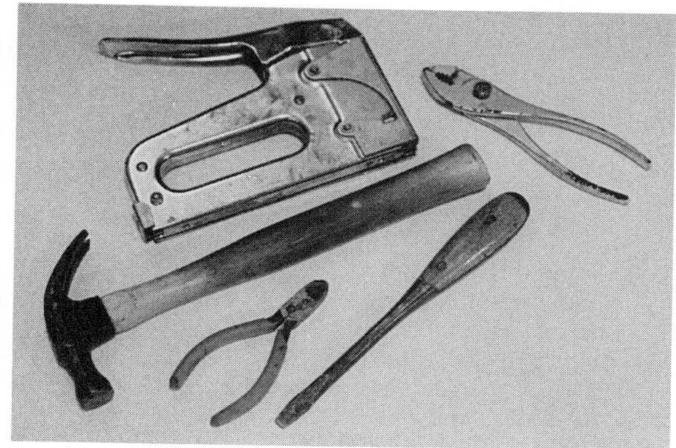

A light-duty rechargeable drill is handy to have.

A stapler, pliers, a small hammer, side-cutters, and a screwdriver round out the tool selection.

Miscellaneous Tools

Other tools you'll need include a set of screwdrivers, a pair of pliers, a pair of side cutters, a small hammer for driving ring nails (if you plan to use them), and a pair of scissors. Tools you may not need, but are handy to have, include a wooden mallet for tapping your chisel and a paint scraper for fast removal of epoxy drips.

Finally, don't start work until you have a pair of safety glasses and a respirator.

Setting Up Shop

You don't need a fancy shop to build a kayak; in fact, on nice days I often move my work outside. What you do need is a space a few feet longer and at least 6 feet wider than the kayak you're building. Your garage, basement, attic, or shed will do if it has sufficient light, ventilation, and electrical power. Many woodworkers already have fully equipped shops that are too short for building a long kayak. In this case, make all the pieces in the shop, then assemble the kayak outside and move it into your hallway or living room at night.

Safety glasses and a respirator—don't start work without them.

Good light is essential when building a kayak; you must be able to judge curves, joints, and surface quality entirely by eye. And you must be certain that the almost colorless epoxy resin is evenly and completely spread over the surfaces to be joined. If your shop isn't well lit, buy a cheap 48-inch fluorescent-light fixture, hang it from the rafters or ceiling, and your problem will be solved.

Building the kayaks in this book involves working with epoxy resins, varnish, paint, and acetone. In addition, copious quantities of sawdust are produced. Breathing in these fumes and particles is both unhealthy and unpleasant. Your shop must have enough doors or windows for good ventilation. If it doesn't, or if you're building during winter, install an exhaust fan. This can simply be a household fan set on a window sill. In any case, use your respirator.

Building a strong pair of sawhorses is a good tune-up project. Pad the tops with a scrap of carpet.

Professional power tools draw considerable amperage. If your shop's electrical power is supplied by an extension cord be sure it's rated for the job. Any extension cord used with these tools should be of at least 14-gauge wire (12-gauge is better); the longer the cord is the more crucial heavy wire becomes. Your tools will still operate if you use a thin cord, but they'll overheat and might burn out.

Epoxy resin should be used within a certain temperature range. During winter or on cold nights, your shop should be heated. In my small, uninsulated shop two portable electric heaters provide sufficient warmth on all but the coldest nights. On very cold nights, you can make a "tent" over your boat from a plastic tarp and aim a heater under it.

Equip the shop with a sturdy set of sawhorses to hold your kayak. Pad the tops of the sawhorses with pieces of scrap carpet, so the boat won't get scratched. You'll need a workbench or table to lay out your plans and to make and assemble smaller parts. Much of kayak building involves just sitting and thinking, so think about getting a stool or chair for your shop.

systems. Another useful thickener is West System 404, a high-density and high-strength filler. It produces a very strong mixture that's useful for bonding rudder mounts, footbraces, and other hardware.

Epoxy, regardless of all its wonderful properties, needs reinforcement when used in highly stressed areas like hull seams. You could use keelsons, butt plates, and chine logs at the seams, but a far simpler and lighter solution is fiberglass tape to reinforce the seams. Fiberglass tape is nothing more than a strip of fiberglass cloth; it's not even sticky. When combined with a plastic resin, such as epoxy, it forms a tough and durable structure; that's basically how fiberglass kayaks are built, after all. Be sure to buy the selvage-type tape and not the sort with unfinished edges. Fiberglass tape may be available in various weights; I prefer 9-ounce tape. It's far more economical to buy tape in 50-yard rolls than by the yard.

Epoxy manufacturers also sell many special-purpose products to mix with resin. These include low- and high-temperature hardeners, graphite powder to produce low-friction surfaces and protect the resin from sunlight (normally, epoxy must be over-coated with paint or varnish), aluminum powder to increase surface hardness, fire-retardant filler, and others. I've used some of these products, but not long enough to recommend them. If you've always wanted a chemistry set, they may be the next best thing.

Having a few inexpensive accessories and supplies makes using epoxy systems much easier. In addition to the dispensing pumps and disposable mixing cups mentioned earlier, you should have stirring sticks, several pairs of disposable gloves, and an apron to keep the sticky stuff off your clothes. For applying epoxy, get disposable brushes, foam rollers, and a plastic squeegee or plastic putty knife. The only truly effective solvent for epoxy is acetone; get some for cleaning up.

Set up a tray or small table—that you don't have any other use for— and use it as your epoxy station. Having all your epoxy-related paraphernalia in one place makes building easier, and you can move it all out of the way after you're finished.

Several manufacturers market epoxy-resin systems formulated for marine woodworking. Over the years I've used West System, System Three, and Evercoat epoxies. I can't say that I prefer any of these brands over another; they all work well. If you work carefully and don't sheath the hull in fiberglass cloth, you'll need two to three quarts of epoxy to build a kayak. But a gallon container usually costs only a few dollars more than two quart-cans, and if you spill any you'll wish you'd spent the extra money.

Epoxy resins, hardeners, and solvents contain potentially dangerous chemicals. Avoid getting them on your skin; wear disposable gloves and use barrier cream. Don't use acetone to remove epoxy from your skin; use soap and water, vinegar, or waterless hand cleaner instead. Even though you might not smell them, epoxy emits fumes—so keep that window open. As epoxy cures, it gives off heat; several ounces of epoxy left sitting in a cup produces enough heat to crack a glass container or melt some types of plastic. Use paper or thick plastic cups for mixing epoxy, and be sure to pour any that's left over into a metal can.

Fasteners

Very few metal fasteners are needed in a plywood kayak. In fact, you could build one of these boats with no metal in it at all. Most kayaks, however, will contain a few screws, ring nails, and some copper wire.

Stainless steel comes in various grades, some of which are not very stainless at all; so, particularly if you'll be paddling in salt water, buy screws from a reputable marine dealer. Bronze ring nails can be used to help hold down the kayak's deck. (These are sometimes called boat nails.) Don't substitute brass or copper fasteners for bronze. They are not nearly as strong or as corrosion-resistant. And please, don't try to save a few cents by using steel or galvanized fasteners—wouldn't you feel foolish with big rust streaks down the side of your kayak? If you use staples, get stainless steel, Monel, or bronze, in case one breaks off in the wood or some aren't removed.

The other metal fastener that will be used is uninsulated copper wire for stitching the hull together. I prefer 18-gauge wire that is sold at many hardware stores for hanging birdfeeders and tying up roses. Copper is the best type of wire to use because it cuts easily and sands

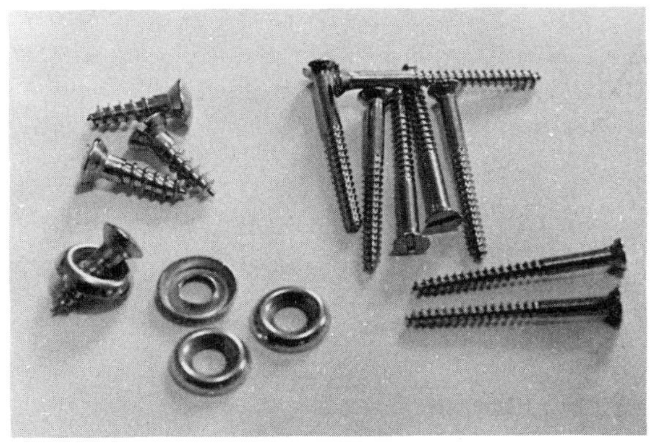

(left) These are all the stainless steel fasteners that go into a kayak. Don't be a cheapskate and substitute brass or galvanized hardware.

(right) Copper wire is used to clamp the hull until the epoxy sets; bronze ring nails hold down the deck until the epoxy sets.

flush with the wood. Stainless steel wire is available but it's very stiff, hard to twist, and very difficult to sand. A few builders use heavy monofilament fishing line because it's almost invisible—but imagine tying all those knots.

Finding Materials

Going to most lumberyards and asking for okoume plywood will result in little more than a funny look from the salesperson. Marine plywoods, epoxies, and fasteners are all specialty items. If you don't live in a traditional boatbuilding area, you'll probably have to order some materials by mail. Ask local boatbuilders where they buy materials or look through the ads in *WoodenBoat* magazine for local sources. There's a list of suppliers who sell by mail in Appendix B.

Chapter 5
The Plans

I drew the plans for the three kayaks in this chapter for my own use. They're not perfect for everyone, but I'll make no excuses for that. I've always drawn plans for kayaks that I wanted to paddle, not necessarily for kayaks that I thought would sell well. I hope from reading my descriptions that you'll be able to judge if one of the kayaks is the sort of boat you want. To that end, I'll try to describe both their flaws and their attributes, but these are subjective. One last caveat: if you want a boat that's not drawn here, then do go out and find the plans or draw them for yourself. Never choose a kayak simply because the plans for it are in front of you, or because you don't want to spend a few dollars on plans for a boat you like better.

It can be frustrating trying to read plans if you're not used to it, or even if you are. I spent several years sitting in my office at a civil engineering firm answering questions from contractors and county inspectors who couldn't understand something in our plans. It drove me to building kayaks. Most people who draw plans really do try to make them easy to understand, but what's obvious to one person is often obtuse to another. Having a good clean set of full-size drawings, the accompanying instructions, and a little patience will answer most questions. Experience will answer many of the rest. The last few questions might require an answer from the designer.

The Yare

"The ducks leave a bigger wake than the Yare," says one paddler after taking her out for a spin.

I designed the predecessor of the Yare, the Skua 16, for the Winter '91 issue of *Sea Kayaker* magazine. Many readers built and enjoyed it.

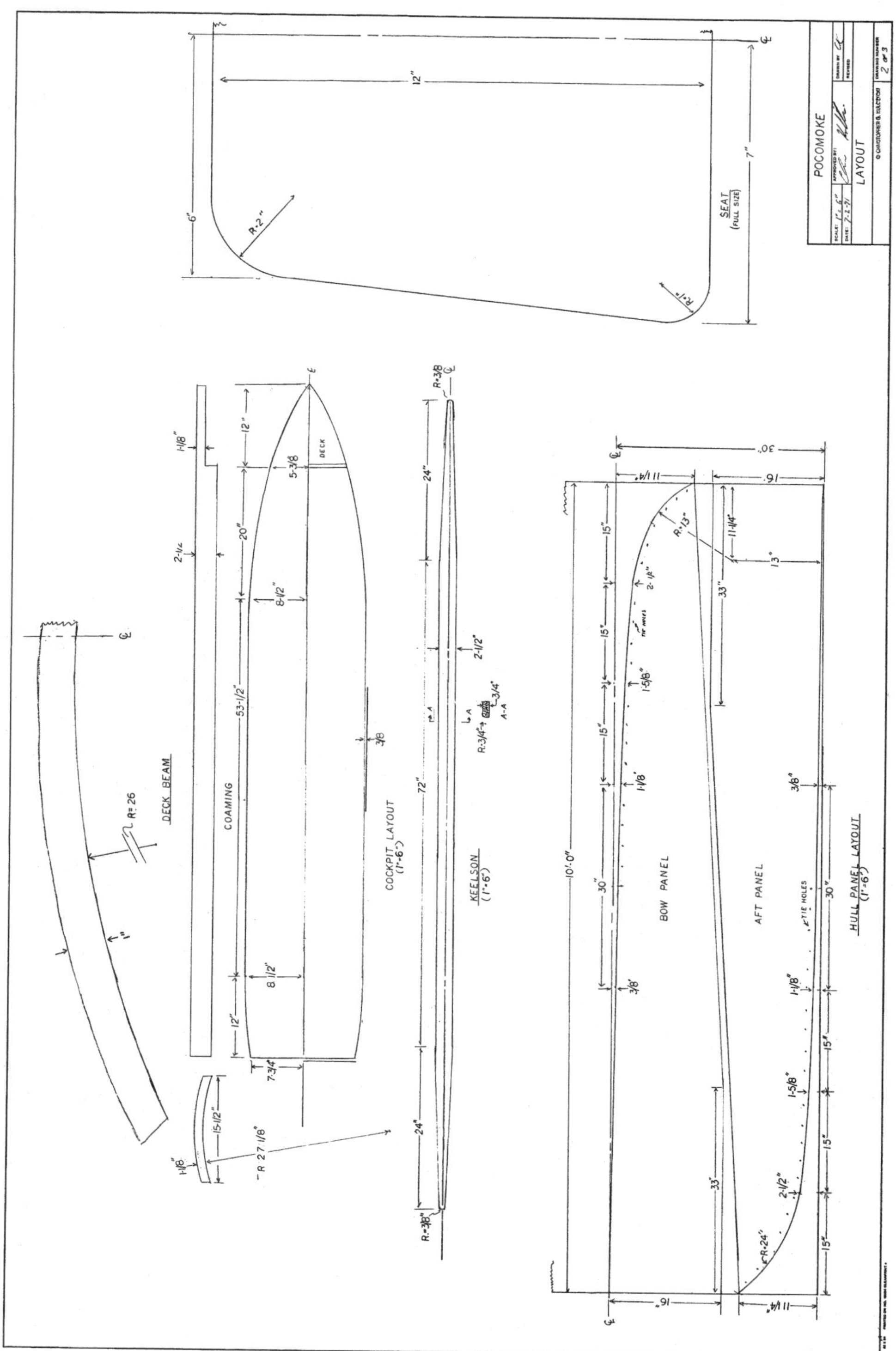
POCOMOKE
LAYOUT
SEAT
(FULL SIZE)
DECK BEAM
COAMING
COCKPIT LAYOUT
(1"=6")
KEELSON
(1"=6")
BOW PANEL
AFT PANEL
HULL PANEL LAYOUT
(1"=6")

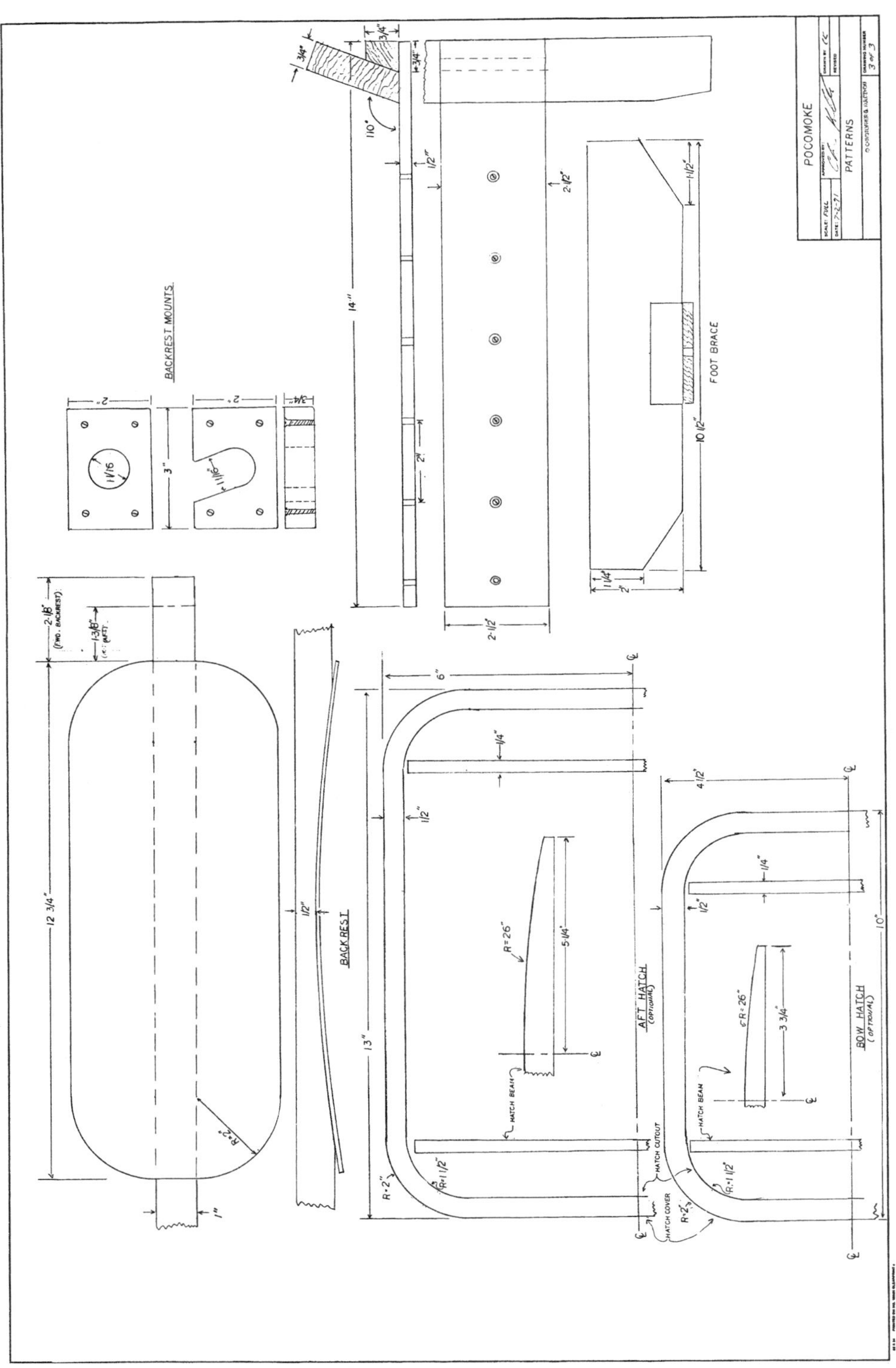
BACKREST MOUNTS
FOOT BRACE
BACKREST
AFT HATCH
(OPTIONAL)
BOW HATCH
(OPTIONAL)
HATCH BEAM
HATCH CUTOUT
HATCH COVER
POCOMOKE
PATTERNS
SCALE: FULL
DATE: 7-2-71
3 OF 3

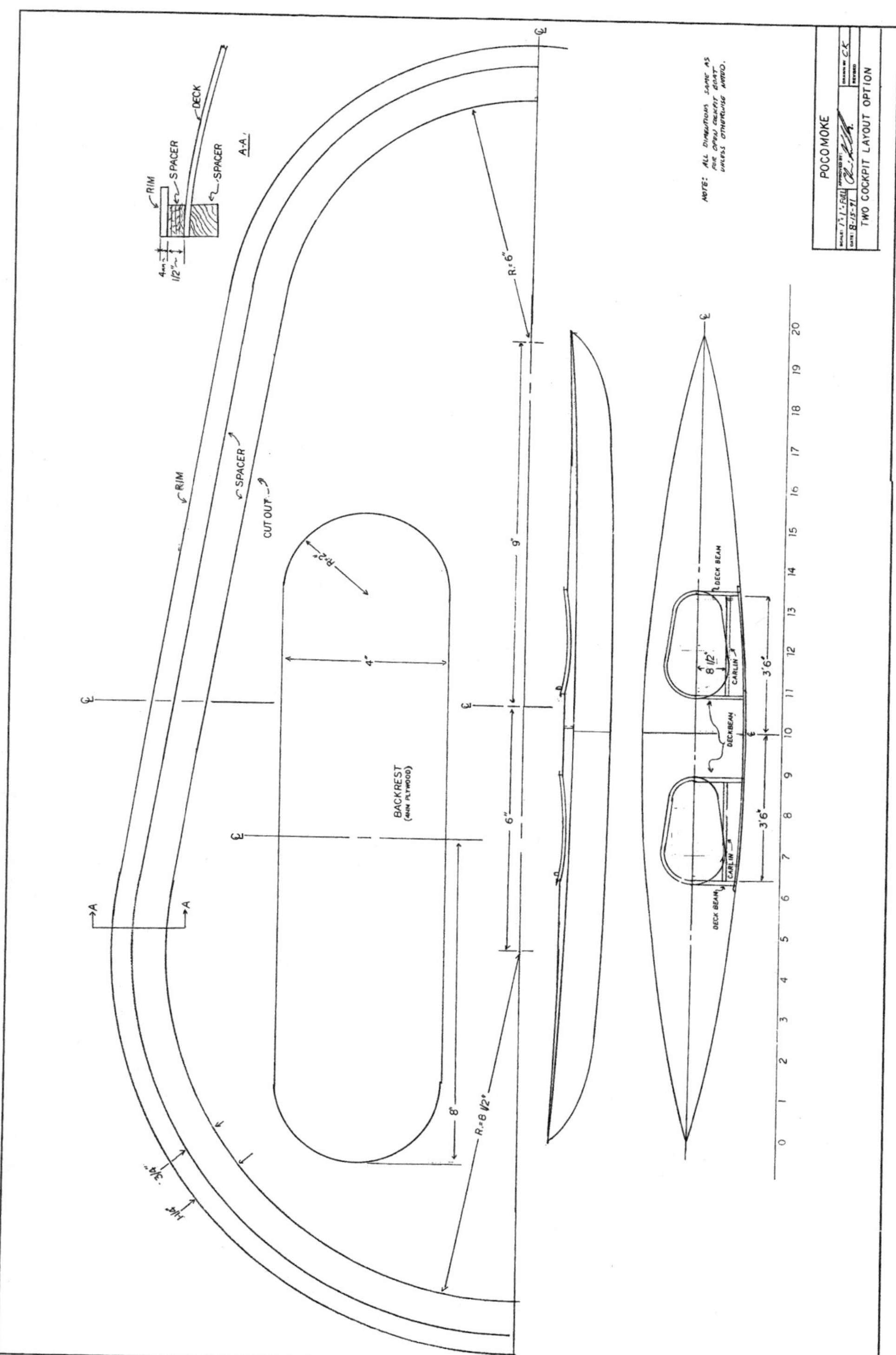
POCOMOKE
TWO COCKPIT LAYOUT OPTION
NOTE: ALL DIMENSIONS SAME AS FOR OPEN COCKPIT BOAT UNLESS OTHERWISE NOTED.
RIM
SPACER
DECK
A-A
CUT OUT
BACKREST (4MM PLYWOOD)
DECK BEAM
CARLIN
DECKBEAM
3'6"
8 1/2"
R.=6"
R.=2"
R.=8 1/2"
9"
6"
4"
8"
3/4"
1/4"

Chapter 6
Making the Hull Panels

Boats are composed of curves. For many woodworkers, this is a daunting fact. After all, you can't just slap down a straightedge and draw a curve. But by using a few tricks, laying out the curved lines of the hull panels is not too difficult. When building a hard-chine boat, such as the Cape Charles, you can even get away with slight errors in your layout. On the other hand, compounded-plywood boats, such as the Yare and the Pocomoke, must have their panels laid out and cut exactly right if they are to "bend up" properly.

In building the Yare or the Pocomoke, all four hull panels will be cut from half a sheet of plywood, then joined with a scarf joint to form two long sections. It's easiest to lay out both panels on one half of the sheet first, then rip it in half, stack the two halves, and cut the panels out.

In building the Cape Charles, the plywood panels are joined with a scarf joint prior to drawing and cutting the panels out. I'll discuss layout first, then scarfing, so you'll need to reverse the order of these steps if you're building the Cape Charles.

Laying Out the Panels

Most kayak plans have layout diagrams showing the exact dimensions of the hull panels. Usually these include offsets from the edge of the plywood sheet or from a baseline. You'll have to transfer these measurements to your plywood sheet and then connect them with a curved or straight line.

Offsets are measurements at right angles to the baseline, centerline, or panel edge. They are points shown as a given distance along the baseline or centerline, then a given distance to the left or right of it.

Mark long baselines or centerlines on the plywood with a straightedge or chalkline. If you don't have a sufficiently long straightedge, the factory-cut edge on another sheet of plywood works fine. When using a chalkline, first shake any excess chalk off the string as you pull it out of its case, otherwise it will splatter when snapped and leave a thick, imprecise line. Always measure from the edge of the chalkline rather than try to estimate its center; of course, you must always use the same edge of the chalkline.

Master boatbuilder Yoachim Russ lays out the panels for a kayak. His batten is held in place with clamps and brads. Notice the long straightedge that marks the top of the panel.

Lay down your measurements with a rafter square to ensure that they are exactly at right angles to the baseline or edge. Mark each measurement point with a small, penciled cross. After you've laid out all the points, double-check them—it's less trouble than ordering more wood if you've goofed.

Use your straightedge to draw any straight lines on the panels, but the curved lines should be drawn with a *batten.* A batten is simply a thin, flexible strip of wood. Lengths of 1- x ¼-inch lath make good battens; ½-inch square spruce is even better. Select a piece that has extremely even grain and no knots. It should bend smoothly and evenly over its entire length. It's worth annoying your local lumberyard by looking through their entire stack for one good batten.

The batten is used like a flexible straightedge. Hold it against the measurement points as you draw the line. You can buy special lead weights, called ducks, to hold the batten in place, or you can drive small brads at each measurement point and hold the batten against these with clamps, a few bricks, or rocks. Take your time adjusting the batten to ensure a fair curve: that is, a curve without any bumps,

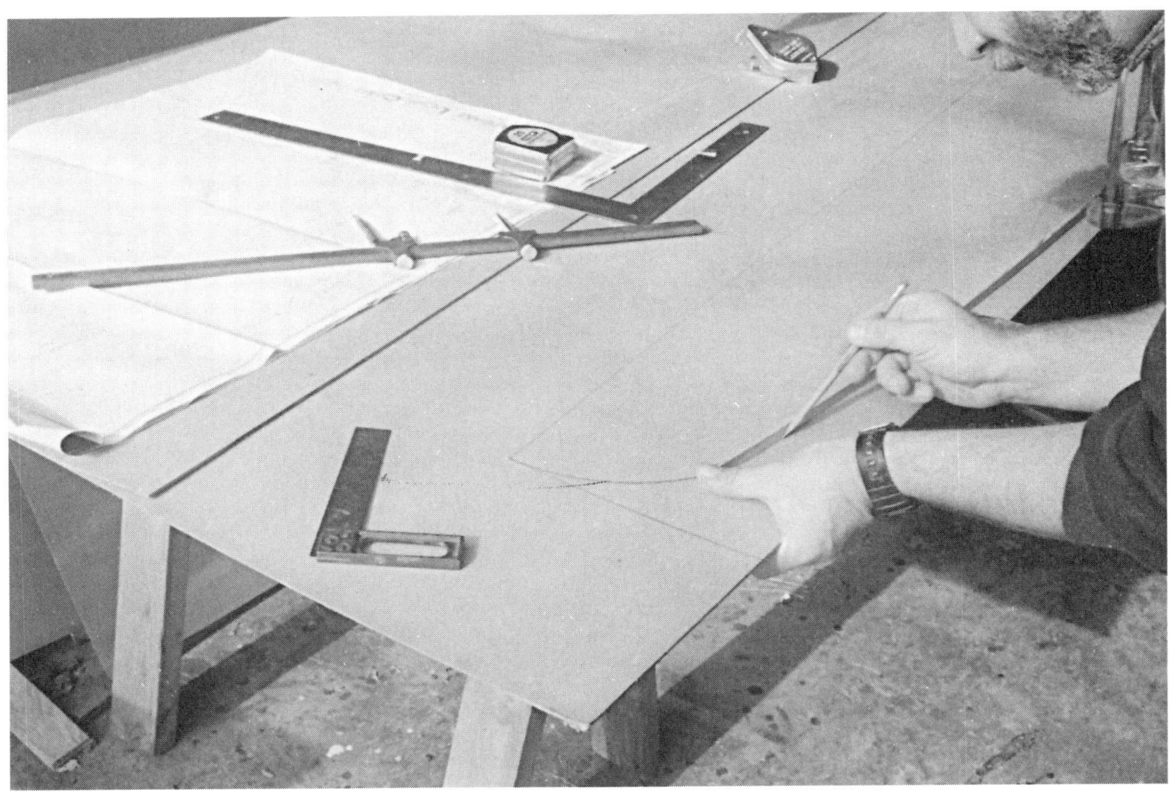

I use a batten to draw a fair curve. I have several battens of different thicknesses that are best for particular curves.

kinks, flat spots, or hollow areas. The only way I know to judge the fairness of a curve is to look down the batten. When you're satisfied that it is laying in a truly fair line, pencil in the curve.

Occasionally, you'll need to lay out a curve or arc by using its radius, which is given on the plan. A curve's radius is simply the distance from the center point of a circle to its perimeter. The best tool for laying out a radial curve is a set of trammels: these are a larger version of a bar compass used in drafting. The trammels are clamped to a wooden bar; one trammel holds a pencil, the other a sharp point. The trammels are adjusted to the proper distance apart and used like a compass. Of course, you can make longer bars and swing larger radii with trammels than with a compass.

If you don't have trammels, draw the curve by tying two small loops in a piece of string; the loops will hold a brad and a pencil at the same distance apart as the radius of the curve being drawn. Drive in the brad at the radius point, keep the string taut, and then swing the arc. Another method is to drill two holes in a strip of scrap wood, using one for the pencil and the other for the brad.

Cutting Out the Panels

Trammels are a type of compass used to draw arcs or parts of a large circle. In this case, the arc forms the after end of the kayak's hull panels.

Now that the hull panels are laid out and all the measurements double-checked, it's time to cut them out. Fit your sabersaw with a fresh 10-tooth-per-inch woodcutting blade. The mirror-image port and starboard sections should be cut from stacked panels to ensure that they will be identical. Lay the plywood on your workbench with the layout line just over the bench's edge. Clamp both panels together so they won't shift as you cut.

Don't cut the panels exactly on the line. If you have a steady hand, try to stay about 1⁄16 inch outside it; if not, aim for about 1⁄8 inch outside it. Later you'll trim the panels exactly to the line with a block plane. Allow the sabersaw to find its best speed through the wood; don't try to push it faster than it can cut. You may find it easier to guide the saw with two hands. Always wear safety goggles so you won't be temporarily blinded by a puff of sawdust. Keep moving the panel on the workbench, so it's always supported an inch or so from where you're cutting.

Hold the sabersaw with both hands and let it find its own speed. Cut just outside your layout line.

Planing the Panels

I prefer to remove the last bit of wood to the layout lines with a block plane instead of with a sabersaw because I'm much less likely to cut beyond the line with the plane. A plane also leaves a fairer curve and a smoother edge. It's important to keep the plane blade sharp and not set too deep. Though it might seem that planing is a tedious step, you can finish off the edges to a set of hull panels in about 20 minutes.

When trimming the cut-out parts, remember that the two sides of the boat must be absolutely, positively, and without doubt identical. If they aren't, the kayak will pull to one side, and you'll spend all your paddling time going in circles. With this in mind, support the panels so they don't droop over the edge of your workbench. Otherwise, the top panel will come out slightly larger than the bottom panel. Try to keep your plane perpendicular to the panels so as not to plane more from one than the other. Sight down the panels as you plane to make sure the edge is fair because it is easy to plane a flat spot. For this reason, it's better to plane to the outside of the pencil line. When you've finished planing, lay the panels on the shop floor and check once again that they're identical.

Use a block plane to trim the panels exactly to the layout lines. Plane the panels in pairs so they'll be identical.

Scarf Joints

Kayaks are generally longer than sheets of plywood. So you'll need to join two or more pieces of plywood to form sheets a little longer than the kayak you intend to build. The best and most elegant way to accomplish this is with a scarf joint, which is two overlapping bevels glued together.

The idea behind a scarf is to provide a large surface for the glue to bond to. If the length of the joint is at least eight times the thickness of the wood, then a properly glued joint will be as strong as the wood. I've purposely broken numerous scarfed panels to see if the scarf was a weak point; in all instances the surrounding wood cracked first.

Cutting a Scarf Using a Block Plane

The simplest way to cut a scarf is with a block plane. Before you start be sure that the plane is sharp. Don't just feel it with your finger; try it out on a piece of plywood. The glue in plywood quickly dulls plane irons, so it might need to be resharpened after cutting a few scarfs. Set your blade for a shallow cut. This is better than planing off great

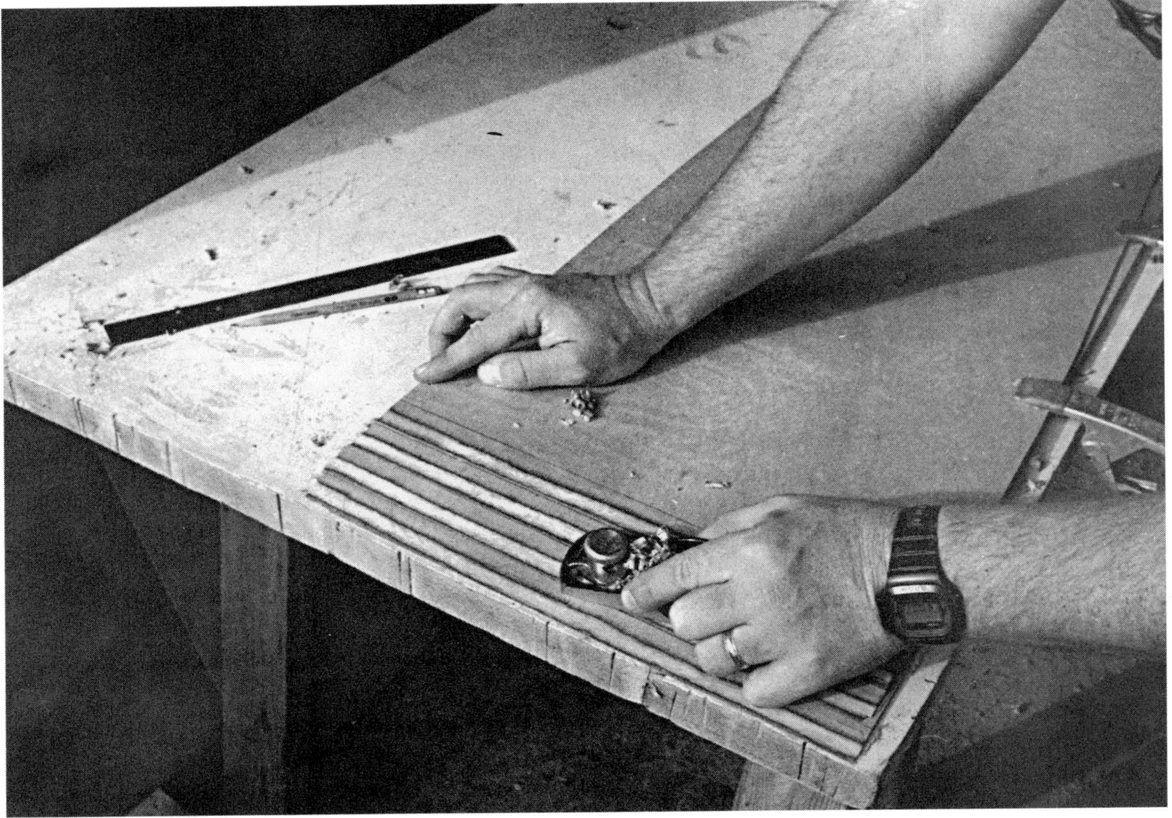

As you cut the scarf, the plywood's veneers will appear as bands. Notice how the four panels are stacked with their edges staggered.

swaths of wood all at once, because sooner or later you will tear out a big chunk and perhaps ruin the panel.

Before planing, the scarf joint has to be marked out. Begin by drawing a line along the joint's inside edge. Since you'll be cutting an 8:1 scarf this line will be one inch from the edge of the wood when joining 3mm plywood (3mm multiplied by 8 is 24mm, or about 1 inch). With 4mm plywood an 8:1 scarf would be 1¼ inches wide.

Line up the edge of the panel to be scarfed flush with the edge of your workbench. If the edge of the workbench is chewed up and scarred, tack down a good surface on it first. You will be removing the wood between the pencil line and the bottom edge of the panel where it meets the workbench. Start by holding the plane at a slight angle and slowly cut along the edge of the plywood. As a "ramp" is formed, the layers in the plywood will appear as bands. Try to keep these bands parallel as you plane. When you have a smooth, flat surface between your pencil line and a feather-like edge against the workbench you're done.

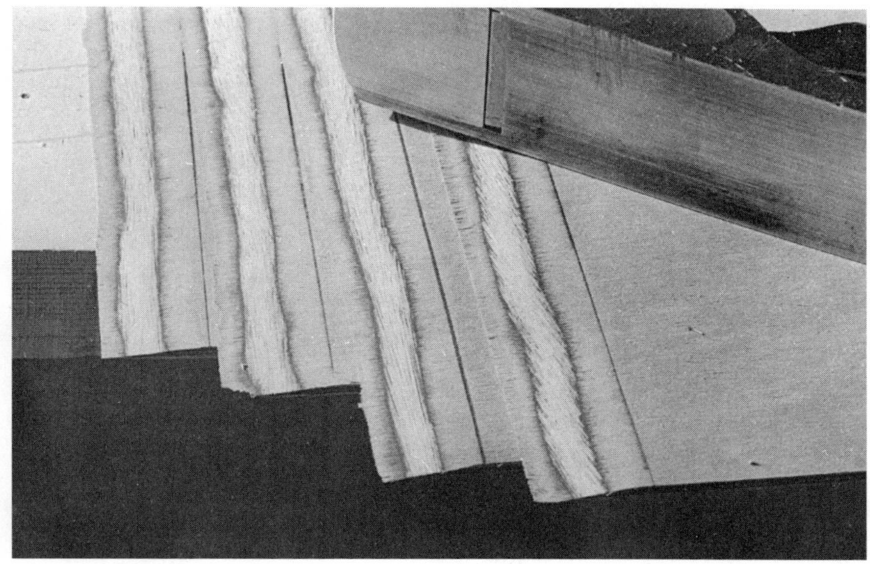

This scarf was cut with a belt sander. It needs to be touched up with a block plane.

To save time, you can cut scarfs on as many as four panels at once. Position the panels flush with the edge of the workbench. Slide the top panel back so that its edge rests on the pencil line of the panel below it; stagger all the panels that you're scarfing in this way and clamp them to the workbench. Now you can cut a ramp between the pencil line on the top sheet and the edge of the workbench, just as you would with a single sheet.

Cutting scarfs with a block plane is probably easier to do than to explain. Practice on a piece of scrap and you'll soon get the hang of it.

Other Ways to Cut Scarfs

Cutting scarfs with a block plane is simple and convenient. But professional boatbuilders, who must be very efficient to make a living, have come up with several time-saving methods for cutting scarfs. If you decide to build more than one kayak, one of these methods is worth trying.

I cut many of my scarfs with a belt sander. The technique is similar to using a block plane. Mark the edge of the scarf and stagger the panels at the edge of your bench. Sand away the wood to form a ramp instead of planing it off. Hold the sander so the belt runs down the ramp, not up or sideways to it. This will keep the plywood from tearing. It's easy to sand off too much wood, so work slowly. An 80-grit sanding belt seems best for cutting scarfs.

Another method I've used requires a router and jig. The router is fitted with a wide mortising bit and mounted on a short board. The board, with the attached router, slides up and down a frame, which is set at the proper angle to cut an 8:1 scarf. The frame, or jig, fits over the plywood panel to be scarfed, and you push the router along to cut a perfect scarf. The only drawback is that the set-up can take as long as cutting the scarf with a plane or belt sander. Of course, a production shop could dedicate a router and table exclusively to scarfing and have an almost perfect system.

I also own a scarfing attachment for my circular saw. It's made by West System and cuts scarfs on panels up to ⅜ inch thick. The attachment consists of a guide that holds the saw at the proper angle to the panel. The device rests against a straightedge that is clamped to the panel. Again, the main drawback is setup time, and it won't handle several panels at once.

Gluing Scarfs

Though I've never heard of one failing, you should always be extra careful when gluing scarf joints. Check that the temperature is within the epoxy manufacturer's specifications, that the resin and hardener are mixed to exactly the right ratio, and double-check that the panels are perfectly aligned.

First, lay the panels to be joined on a flat surface with a sheet of plastic under the scarf. Mix an ounce or two of epoxy and thicken it to the consistency of honey. Spread some epoxy on both bevels. Carefully position the bevels and check that the panel is straight by stretching a string beside it. Cover the joint with a second sheet of plastic.

Clamping a scarf joint can be tricky. With very narrow panels or solid-wood strips, ordinary C-clamps will do the job, but with wider scarfs you have to be more creative. The easiest method is to use staples: lay a strip of thin scrap plywood over the plastic-covered joint

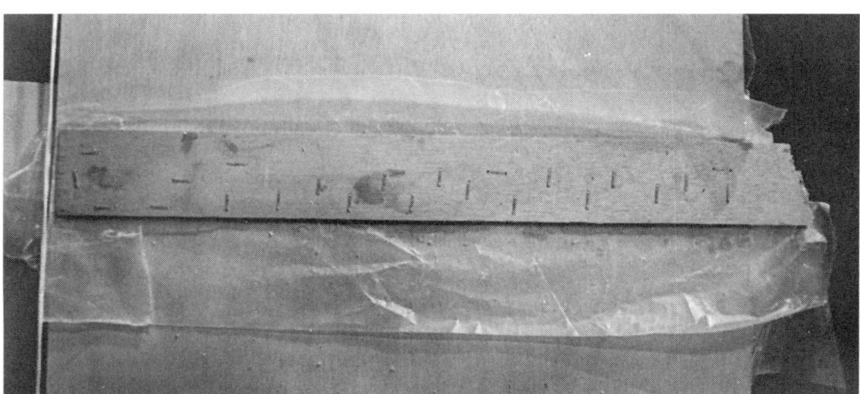

Clamping the scarf by stapling it to the work surface is quick and easy. The piece of scrap plywood will be pulled up with all the staples when the epoxy has cured. The string line running alongside the panels is used to check alignment.

easiest to glue the sheer clamps onto both hull panels at once. That way, you can ensure that they are identically positioned, and you'll need only half as many clamps.

Start by stacking the panels back-to-back with the eventual outside faces turned in. Spread thickened epoxy along the entire length of both sheer clamps. Then, place them in the proper position on the hull and, every foot or so, clamp them together.

Clamp both sheer clamps to the plywood at once by laying the panels back-to-back.

At the cockpit area of the Yare and the Pocomoke, bend the sheer clamps to curve smoothly between the two straight sections. There will be two spots at either end of this area where the sheer clamps won't follow exactly the tops of the panels. At these points, the plywood will be planed off later. Wait overnight for the epoxy to cure before moving on to the next step.

Installing sheer clamps requires lots of clamps. If you don't own enough, borrow them from friends and neighbors or buy inexpensive 2-inch C-clamps.

Stitching and Taping

The stitch-and-tape assembly method solves the problem of trying to hold the hull panels into the shape of a kayak with conventional woodworking clamps. By tying the hull together with short lengths of copper wire, the large panels can be held in position while fiberglass tape and epoxy are applied to permanently join the seams. In the following section, I'll go over the basic stitching and taping techniques and then describe the exact sequence used to join the Yare's, Pocomoke's, and Cape Charles's hulls.

First, drill holes for the wire along the seam to be joined. They should be a little larger than the diameter of the wire used (about 1/16 inch for 18-gauge wire). The holes should be about 1/4 inch from the plank's edge and about 4 inches apart. It's best to stack, and then drill

Drill holes for the tie wires every 4 inches. Wire the panels together with short pieces of copper wire.

Twist the tie wires on the outside of the hull. Don't overtighten them or they will break or tear through the wood.

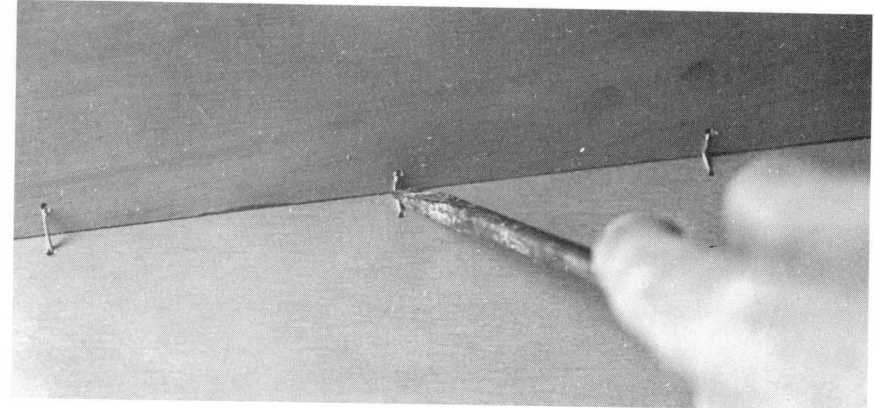

Push each wire flat against the inside seam with the point of a screwdriver. This tightens the wires and eliminates little bumps under the tape.

identical panels together, so the holes will be in matching positions.

Next, align and stitch the panels together. Cut wire into 3-inch lengths, pass the pieces through the holes, and twist the wires finger tight on the outside of the hull. Obviously, it's easier to do this with the hull upside down. When all the wire ties are in place and finger tight, tighten them further with a pair of pliers, but only until the panels touch.

Overtightening will pull the wire through the wood or break it. If some areas are difficult to pull together, drill a few more holes for additional ties. Pay careful attention to the curve of the seam; is it fair? If not, adjust the ties or remove them and touch up the panels with your plane. Finally, flip the hull over and, using a screwdriver point, push down each wire so it lies flat against the inside seam.

As you wire the boat's bow and stern together, you'll have to stop and cut a bevel in the sheer clamps, so they'll meet at a point. Make

The sheer clamps are beveled to meet in a point. This is a tricky step, so take your time. Notice the tie wire under the bow.

this tricky cut carefully with your handsaw. Cut the sheer clamps a little proud and then plane them until they fit perfectly. After you've wired the bow and stern together, check that the hull is symmetrical. If the panels are misaligned by even an ⅛ inch, the boat could pull to one side. Run a string line down the center of the hull, and use your square to check that both sides of the hull are equidistant from it. If the hull is twisted, push it into shape.

Start taping the seams by mixing some epoxy, thickening it to the consistency of caulk, and apply a bead of it on each seam. Smooth down the bead so it forms a fillet just covering the tie wires.

Epoxy manufacturers sell disposable syringes that make it easy to apply an even epoxy bead. Another neat way to apply a bead of epoxy is to cut the corner off a Ziploc-type plastic bag and push a small piece of plastic tube through it. Tape the tube into place and pour some thickened epoxy into the bag. Squeeze the bag to lay down a bead of epoxy on the seams.

Cut a piece of fiberglass tape to the required length, and lay it on the seam. Mix some more epoxy, but don't thicken it; brush it onto the tape, saturating it and the wood below. Apply another layer of tape and saturate it, likewise a third layer, if the building instructions call for it. It's best to stagger the tape, side to side, by a fraction of an inch so the edges don't line up and cause a hard spot. Also, stagger the ends by a couple of inches. Using a jabbing motion with your brush, work any air bubbles or dry spots out of the tape. Mix and brush on more epoxy as you need it, until the fiberglass is thoroughly saturated; it should be translucent with no opaque areas remaining.

I use a plastic bag like a pastry decorator to spread a bead of epoxy along each seam. The spout is a piece of ¼-inch plastic tubing taped to a hole in the bag.

Lay the tape onto each seam; the bead of epoxy will hold it in place until you wet it out.

However, avoid brushing on more epoxy than required: it will add needless and expensive weight but little strength. If you plan to epoxy-saturate the hull's interior, you can do it now. Just brush two thin coats of epoxy onto all the exposed wood inside the hull; but don't coat the outside of the hull yet.

Once the epoxy has cured, gently turn the hull upside down and cut off the wire ties. Scrape or sand off any epoxy that's dripped through the seam. With a pair of side cutters, cut off the wires almost flush to the wood, so that only a minimal amount of sanding and planing will be required to smooth the joint. Remember that if you varnish your hull, this seam will be visible, so sand or plane it carefully.

Work all the air bubbles and dry spots out of the epoxy with a disposable brush. This is a good time to seal the inside of the hull.

When the epoxy inside the hull has cured, flip the boat over and cut off the wire ties. Then sand or plane the seams.

Use only unthickened epoxy on the outside of the boat. Lay the tape over the seam as before, then saturate it and work all the air bubbles out of the tape. Apply a second layer of tape, if required by the plans, and work the bubbles out of it. When the epoxy has started to harden, brush on one or two more coats to fill the tape's weave.

Tape the outside seams as you did the inside. A disposable bristle brush works better than the roller I'm using here.

Unlike paint and varnish, epoxy is best overcoated before it's fully hardened. The chemical bond between a fresh coating and a partially cured coat is very strong, so there's no need to sand between coats of epoxy, if less than 72 hours have elapsed since the previous coat was applied.

Occasionally, the tape won't lie flat on the hull. This often happens where it passes over sharp corners, such as at the bow and stern. One way to correct the problem is by draping plastic wrap over the wet tape and pushing it into the epoxy; the tape will be held down, and the plastic will peel off easily after the epoxy has hardened.

The two panels of a Yare's hull are ready to be wired together. They are clamped to a board under the scarf to help keep them aligned.

Joining the Hulls

In this section, I'll apply the stitch-and-tape method to our three boats. This is the only step where the techniques used to build the Yare, the Pocomoke, and the Cape Charles differ substantially. Follow these separate descriptions for joining the hull of the boat you're building.

Joining the Yare's Hull

The Yare's hull is probably the trickiest of the three to join. Since there are no keelson or chines to keep the hull rigid while it's being put together, the builder must "eyeball" the proper shape. And while it's being initially taped, the panels will have little resemblance to the final hull shape.

Start by drilling tie-wire holes along the keel line. Then lay the twin hull panels on your sawhorses; the sheer clamps are up, and keel lines are touching at the scarf. The center eight feet of the two panels will be wired together and taped first. However, you'll notice that the panels don't touch over much of their length. But if you push down near the center of the panels, they'll bend into a shallow "U" and come together.

Wire the panels together for 4 feet to either side of the scarf. Twist the wires loosely on the outside of the boat while pushing the panels down. They must be almost flat across the scarf joint when they are taped. You can hold the panels in this alignment by sliding a scrap board under the scarf joint and clamping the sheer edges to it. Before clamping, place small spacers, about ¾ inch thick, between the sheer edges and the board. The spacers introduce a shallow V that adds rigidity to the boat. The ends of the panels, supported by the sawhorses, should now be considerably higher than the center part of the hull, which will droop down about 2 feet.

When stitched together, the ends of the panels must be higher than the middle. The weight of a full gallon-can of epoxy holds the panels in position so I can tighten the stitches.

Tighten the tie wires so the two panels touch along an 8-foot length. Then, with a screwdriver point, push the wires flat against the seam on the inside. It's particularly important with the Yare that the center seam runs in a smooth curve without any bumps, flat spots, or hollows. Even a slight imperfection will be greatly magnified when the hull is pulled together. Don't hesitate to cut your wire ties and touch up the panel edges with a plane or sandpaper if they aren't perfect. A few extra minutes spent getting this seam just right can save you extra work later on.

The center seam will initially be joined with three layers of fiberglass tape on the inside and one on the outside. Mix up a few ounces of thickened epoxy and spread a bead over the joint. It should just cover the tie wires and fill any gaps between the panels. Lay an 8-foot piece of fiberglass tape over the seam. Mix an additional 8 ounces of epoxy, but don't thicken it.

The Cape Charles's two side panels are wired together first; then the bottom is wired to them. A spreader stick holds the sides to the proper beam measurement.

Now, wire the two bottom panels loosely together along the center seam with the wire twists on the outside of the hull. Lay the bottom panels on the overturned side panels. Drill tie holes along the outside edge of the bottom panels that correspond with the holes you drilled previously in the side panels. Wire the bottom panels to the side panels, again with the wires twisted on the outside of the hull.

The Cape Charles's maximum beam is located 9 feet 6 inches from the tip of the bow. At this point, use a spreader stick to make the kayak's maximum beam at the gunnel 25½ inches and with a second stick, push out the beam at the chine to 21 inches. If these measurements are correct the hull will assume its proper shape, except at the ends. Near the bow and stern, where all four panels meet, the bottom tends to flatten out. Use a clamp to squeeze them into a V shape; the angle should be as drawn in section A-A on page 1 of the plans.

Three pieces of tape come together at the Cape Charles's bow and stern; it will take a little time to get this nice and smooth.

Check the seams for any bumps or hollows and adjust the ties to eliminate them. Now gently turn the hull over (rightside up). The hull must now be carefully supported, otherwise it will be distorted where it rests on the sawhorses or workbench. Push down the tie wires inside the hull and fill the seams with a bead of thickened epoxy. Apply a strip of tape to each of the three inside seams. Saturate the tape, apply second strips, and saturate them.

When the epoxy has hardened, turn the hull over and cut off all the wire ties. Sand or plane the seams, making them smooth and slightly rounded. Apply two layers of tape to each of the three outside seams, using only unthickened epoxy.

Finally, put your hull aside for 12 hours while the epoxy cures. Congratulate yourself: you've completed the hardest step in building your kayak.

Chapter 8
Installing the Deck

A kayak's deck is its most visible part; the deck is what you see when paddling and what others will see first when they look at your boat. You'll certainly want to varnish your deck to show off the wood, so try especially hard to do a neat, clean job of installing it. A minor flaw on the hull can always be hidden with a little fairing compound and a good paint job, but every scratch, dent, and tear in the deck shows.

But since you've already completed the hull, your woodworking skills are tuned up, and installing the deck will be easier for you than building the hull. Working on the deck is an exciting step: you'll finally have an idea of what the finished boat will look like. Even though there will still be a lot to do, it will all seem downhill once the deck is in place.

Before building the deck, you'll have to install the structure that gives it shape and support. This includes making and fitting the deck beams and carlins, and planing the tops of the sheer clamps. You may also want to install bulkheads and backing plates for a rudder before the hull is buttoned up.

The Deck Beams

The deck beams span the hull forward and aft of the cockpit. They support the deck and coaming, help hold the hull at the proper beam, and add rigidity to the kayak. The beams for our three kayaks are curved, or cambered, like the decks. They are made by laminating thin spruce or pine strips over a simple jig.

The radius of a beam describes its curvature: smaller means more curve and a higher deck; larger means less curve and a flatter deck. The radii of the deck beams for our three kayaks are shown on the plans. The Cape Charles and the Yare have 3mm plywood decks; the maximum radius I like to use for 3mm decks is 16 inches. Bending the deck to a radius smaller than this is difficult to do without causing the fasteners at the deck's edges to tear through the wood or the plywood to crack. For boats with a 4mm plywood deck, such as the Pocomoke, a deck radius of around 20 inches is the maximum I would attempt.

If you'd like to increase the volume of your kayak or gain extra knee room, there's no harm in decreasing the deck beam's radius slightly,

Use a simple jig, like this one, to make laminated deck beams. Wrap the deck beam in plastic, so it won't be glued to the jig.

though the appearance of the boat will change. My preference for single kayaks is an 18-inch radius forward and a 24-inch radius behind the cockpit. The transitional area between the two different deck cambers worries some builders. But given the flexibility of 3mm plywood, the deck panels blend together nicely. On doubles, decked with 4mm plywood, I find a 26-inch radius most pleasing to the eye. The camber of the deck does not have to be radial: you could draw it as a section of a parabola or a combination of two radii.

Making the Deck Beams

The deck beams for single kayaks should be about ¾-inch thick and for doubles about 1-inch thick. Lattice 1¼ x ¼ inches makes perfect stock for laminating deck beams, and it's readily available at lumberyards. Cut the lattice into strips a few inches longer than the deck beam. There are three strips for each ¾-inch-thick deck beam and four strips for 1-inch deck beams.

A butt plate reinforces the joint between the two deck panels.

sors. Fold the template down its center line to check that it's symmetrical. If the plans you're using include a full-size drawing of the cockpit opening, you can simply cut it out to use as a template.

Cut a small hole in the deck, about in the center of where the cockpit will be. Insert your tape measure through this hole and measure from the hole to the deck beams and carlins; mark their location on the deck. Position the cockpit template on the deck and center it between the deck beams and the carlins. Mark the opening on the plywood and cut it out with your sabersaw.

After you've cut the cockpit opening, glue butt plates under the deck joint. These are simply little rectangles cut from scrap plywood that span the joint to reinforce it. They should be about two inches long and as wide as the distance between the sheer clamp and the cockpit opening or carlin.

Finally, stand back and admire your boat.

Chapter 9
The Coaming, Seat, and Footbraces

Adding the coaming, seat, and footbraces finally turns your hull and deck into a kayak. Give these parts the attention they deserve because they directly affect your comfort. Seats, footbraces, and, in some cases, coamings, are not structural parts of the kayak, so you can modify them, design your own, or substitute commercially made versions.

Coamings

In addition to being functional, the coaming can be an eye-catching feature. You can make a simple but strong flat plywood coaming, or you can show off your joinery skills with a solid wood or bent-wood coaming.

The size of the coaming is important: if its opening doesn't fit a spray skirt that you can buy, you'll have to make one. The right size coaming will also allow you to raise your knees while sitting in the kayak yet enable you to brace them under the deck.

I'll describe how to make the two types of coamings shown on the plans for our three boats plus another coaming that can be adapted to many kayaks.

Making a Flat Laminated Coaming

The coamings for the Yare, the Cape Charles, and the two-cockpit version of the Pocomoke designs are made by laminating a ring of ¼-inch plywood onto a spacer that's glued to the kayak's deck. This is the most common type of coaming on wooden kayaks. It's popular because it's strong and easy to make. The coamings shown on the plans will accommodate many popular brands of spray skirts; you could, however, easily change the dimensions to accommodate odd-size skirts or odd-size paddlers.

The first step in making a flat, laminated coaming is cutting the spacer the rim will be glued to. Make the spacer from ½-inch plywood, which can be exterior grade since it's barely visible and is sealed with epoxy. The spacer can also be made from two layers of the ¼-inch plywood that was used for the rim, or from four layers of left-over

3mm plywood. It's more economical to cut the spacer in two pieces and lay out the two pieces so they "nest." This way you'll avoid ending up with a large useless piece of wood, cut out of the center of a one-piece spacer.

The coaming's top ring or rim should be made from ¼-inch plywood. I usually use lauan. Marine-grade lauan looks a bit better than exterior grade, but both hold up well. Of course, you could use any waterproof ¼-inch plywood, or even solid wood; how about a zebra wood coaming rim? If you tend to abuse your kayaks, laminate on a second ring or sheath the rim with fiberglass cloth to increase its strength.

After the spacer and rim are ready, spread thickened epoxy on both sides of the spacer and position it on your kayak. Next, set the rim on top of the spacer. Clamp the pieces into place after inserting pads of scrap plywood between the clamps and the rim. This keeps the wood from being dented. Wipe up any epoxy that's squeezed out under the rim; otherwise, the spray skirt will catch on gobs of hard epoxy.

Once the epoxy has cured, sand the inside of the cockpit opening. If you weren't precise when you cut the pieces, there will be lots

The Yare and Cape Charles's coamings are laminated from rings of plywood. The top ¼-inch-thick ring is a little wider than the bottom ½-inch-thick ring, thus forming a lip for a spray skirt.

of sanding before the inside is smooth and even; a rasp or belt sander will knock down the really rough sections. When you're finished, the inside of the opening should show a handsome pattern of plywood layers. Brush a coat of unthickened epoxy onto the exposed edges of plywood around the coaming; after it's soaked in, brush on a second coat.

Making the Pocomoke's Coaming

When drawing the plans for the Pocomoke, I was aware that this type of boat would usually be paddled without a spray skirt. Since I was planning to use it as a platform to take nature photographs, I designed it with a large open cockpit. I also knew from paddling other doubles that the occasional motorboat wake or rogue wave would wash it's deck, so I designed a coaming that's higher than the one on my Klepper to better deflect boarding waves. The coaming has a small overhanging rim for a custom-sewn spray skirt when conditions get rough. This rim is also effective in deflecting water that washes up the coaming.

The spruce coaming on the Pocomoke is functional and handsome. But it's harder to make than a plywood coaming and can crack.

The Pocomoke's coaming can be made from ³⁄₈-inch solid wood, such as spruce or mahogany, or from ¹⁄₄-inch plywood. For solid wood, you'll need to rip it to ³⁄₈-inch-thick stock or have your lumberyard run it through a thickness planer.

Cut the wood into two 2½-inch strips, then lay out and cut the notch at the coaming's forward end as shown in the plans. Before trimming the coaming's after end, trial fit it to ensure a tight fit. Cut out the banana-shaped third piece of the coaming, which fits at the cockpit's after end, with your sabersaw. Check that everything fits; when you're satisfied, glue the coaming to the carlins and deck. It will take quite a few clamps to hold the wood in place. The forward tip of the coaming can be tricky to join, and you'll need to cut another bevel there.

One-quarter-inch plywood can also be used for bulkheads. But plywood bulkheads are more trouble to fit; you can't squeeze them into place as you can foam.

If you're installing the bulkheads while building your boat, fit them after the deck beams and carlins are in place. If retrofitting an existing boat, cutting the hatch openings first makes it easier to fit the bulkheads.

The shape of the bulkheads will depend on their position. Some paddlers prefer the after bulkhead be directly behind the seat; others like enough room behind the seat to carry spare clothes, a lunch, and other supplies. The position of the forward bulkhead is determined largely by the length of your legs.

Start by making cardboard templates that fit in the position of the bulkheads. If you're installing foam bulkheads, the template need not be particularly accurate, since you'll cut the foam ¼ inch or so oversize and squeeze it into place for a perfect fit. Templates for plywood bulkheads, on the other hand, must be as accurate as possible. When you're satisfied with the fit and position of the templates, trace their shapes onto the foam or plywood. Cut closed-cell foam to shape with a large serrated knife or with your sabersaw fitted with a very long blade; cut plywood bulkheads as you would a hull panel. Foam bulkheads are pushed into place and glued with 3M 5200 marine caulk. Plywood bulkheads should be glassed as if taping a hull seam.

If you're installing bulkheads in a boat that will be used only for short day-trips, hatches may be unnecessary. However, some means of ventilating the ends of the kayak is necessary to allow moisture to evaporate. The simplest solution is to drill a large hole in each bulkhead that can be plugged with a cork or dowel when the boat is used; this plug should be removed when the boat is stored. Another approach is to install a marine-type inspection plate (available at marine stores) on each bulkhead; these have the added advantage of allowing small items to be stored in the bow and stern compartments. Of course, the plates should be removed whenever the boat is stored.

Hatches

Hatches are necessary to allow access to the areas behind the bulkheads. However, many hatches are not completely waterproof; the ones I've designed for my boats aren't waterproof. But before you return this volume to your bookseller in disgust, let me assure you that the vast majority of the hatches on plastic and fiberglass kayaks are not completely waterproof either. This isn't as tragic as it sounds because prudent paddlers will keep their gear in waterproof cases and dry-bags. In a day of paddling, the few ounces of water that find their way past most hatches will not noticeably affect the kayak's buoyancy, but your new Nikon will definitely be ruined. It's always safer to assume that any hatch leaks.

If you insist on truly watertight hatches, you can install those ugly plastic marine inspection plates; they even come in rectangular and clear models now. Or you can use the excellent, though equally ugly, British VCP rubber hatches. These are available as kits consisting of the hatch cover and a rim; they are for fiberglass kayaks, but they can be easily adapted to a wooden deck.

This hatch cover may not be 100 percent watertight, but it does a surprisingly good job. The seal is just closed-cell foam weather stripping, like you'd use on your windows.

Two nylon straps with Fastex buckles hold the hatch in place.

The hatch covers used for all three of our boats are identical. They are squares of plywood that are glued to frames with the same camber as the deck's. Wide weather stripping that's glued to the hatch cover's perimeter seals the hatch cover to the deck. Nylon straps screwed to the deck and sheer clamps hold the hatch covers in place.

The plans in Chapter 5 contain templates for the bow- and after-hatch cutouts. (You'll have to redraw them at full scale if you are using only the plans reproduced in this book.) Draw a light centerline on the deck in the area of the hatches. Line up the centerlines on the templates with the centerline on the boat and trace the cutouts. Drill a starter hole for your sabersaw blade, then cut out the openings. Remember, foam bulkheads are 3 inches thick; don't cut into them.

Make two frames for each hatch cover from short pieces of lattice, tracing the curve of the deck onto the lattice strips and cutting them to shape with a sabersaw. The frames should just fit into the deck opening. Glue the hatch frames onto the bottom of the hatch covers with thickened epoxy resin. The frames fit athwartship about 1½ inches from the edge of the hatch cover; use several clamps to hold the hatch cover to the frames. Fore-and-aft frames, sort of minicarlins, can be added to further stiffen the hatch cover.

Glue the foam weather stripping (bought at hardware or autoparts stores) underneath the perimeter of the hatch cover, as shown in the photo on page 114. Use the thickest and widest weather stripping you can find; ¼- x ⅜-inch closed-cell, self-adhesive weather stripping is my current favorite.

After the deck has been varnished, attach the hatch straps to the sheer clamps with ¾-inch screws and finish washers. The straps should be about two feet long so that they can be extended to hold down bulky gear stowed on deck. Fold about 1 inch of each strap over itself and melt the screw hole in it with a nail heated over a flame. Screw the straps into the sheer clamp so that the straps lay on the hatch covers. Finally, attach the buckles to the straps.

Another attractive hatch design seen on wooden kayaks consists of a hatch cover the same size as the hatch cut-out. This type of hatch rests on, and seals to, a frame glued to the underside of the deck. It can be designed to fit perfectly flush with the deck, giving the kayak a very sleek appearance. Hatches of this type are usually held closed by small swiveling latches, as seen in the photos.

If you're designing your own kayak, give the placement of the hatches some thought: when the hatches are located near the bulkheads, the deck in this area will remain quite stiff, but it will be diffi-

This flush-type hatch is on a South Shore Boatworks' 17-foot Sea Tamer kayak. Note the fiberglass seat unit.

cult to reach gear that's slid to the ends of the boat. On the other hand, if the hatches are located farther toward the kayak's ends, the deck loses some rigidity, but it's easier to reach the gear in the bow and stern.

Rudders

Rudders and rudder kits are available from many kayak shops and mail-order catalogs. They are usually designed to be retrofitted to a specific model of plastic or fiberglass kayak, but with a little fiddling, they can usually be adapted to a wooden kayak. I favor Feathercraft and Aquaterra rudders, which are very similar to each other in appearance and operation.

Rudder Mounts

Just locating a rudder mount that fits your kayak might be the biggest obstacle to installing a rudder. If possible, find the mount before installing the deck. If it is to be screwed to the hull, then backing plates should be glued into position before putting down the deck.

Manufacturers of plastic and fiberglass kayaks have specially designed metal mounts fabricated to fit their hulls. Scour the local kayak shops for a mount that's designed for another boat but that might fit yours. Welded mounts that are a close fit can often be bent

Much of the work in installing a rudder is figuring out how to mount it. The rudder mount farthest from the camera was made for a plastic kayak but fits this Yare when faired in with a little epoxy. The kayak closest to the camera has its rudder mounted in a hole that is drilled through the kayak's reinforced stern.

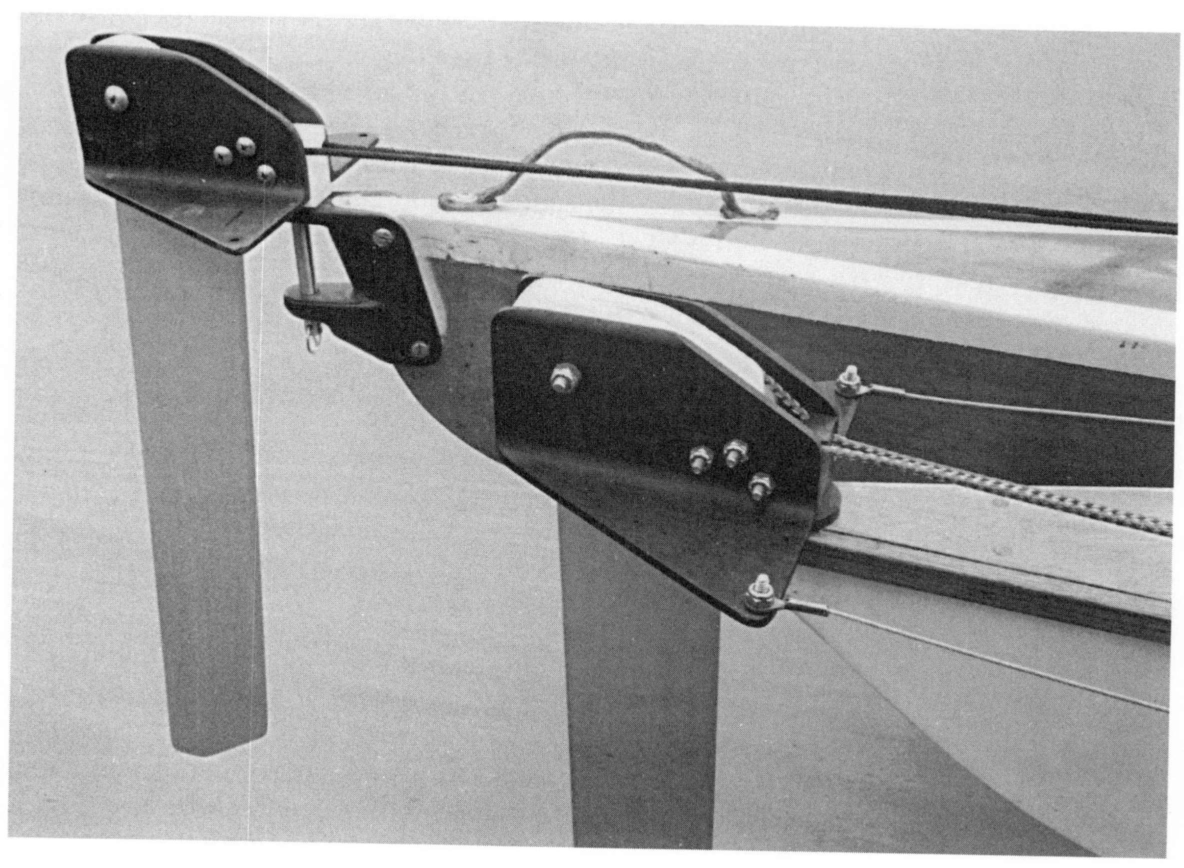

to fit. Cast mounts can sometimes be padded for a perfect fit. West Systems, the epoxy manufacturer, sells a high-strength filler (#404) that I've used to "sculpt in" rudder mounts for a custom fit. The cast-aluminum rudder mount in the photo is intended for an Aquaterra Chinook, but with a little epoxy magic it fits my wife's Yare—not perfectly, but it works.

A machinist or welder you know might be convinced to make a mount to your specifications. You could hire a machine shop to make one for you, but that might be expensive. Another option is to use stainless steel gudgeons that marine stores sell for mounting rudders on small sailing dinghies. With a little bending, these can be adapted to fit many kayaks.

A third option, and my favorite, is to forget about a separate mount and drill a hole in the deck and sheer clamps to accept the rudder pintle (or pin). To do this, cut off the last inch or so of the kayak. Drill a hole the same size as the pintle through the sheer clamps. It must be far enough forward of the newly truncated stern to let the rudder swing freely. Now this is the fun part: to prevent water from entering through this hole and to strengthen the mount, fill the end of the kayak with epoxy. Stand the kayak on end by leaning it against a tree or building; seal the hole you drilled with clear tape and pour in epoxy through the aft hatch or cockpit. Pour in the epoxy an ounce or two at a time; a large mass of curing resin can produce enough heat to melt the tape off the end of the hull! Continue adding epoxy until it's above the level of the mounting hole; you can see the level through the clear tape. When the epoxy has cured, redrill the hole and mount your rudder.

This type of mount will wear and have a sloppy fit after a few seasons. This can be remedied by brushing a little resin inside the hole with a cotton swab and then redrilling the hole. For an improved version, drill the hole a little oversized and glue in a bushing. The bushing can be a short length of metal tubing with the same inside diameter as the pintle's diameter, or your local machine shop can probably make a bronze bushing for a few dollars.

Cables and Deck Hardware

Mounting the rudder is only half the job; now you must run the steering cables, fit the rudder lifting line, and install sliding footbraces.

The steering cable housings will penetrate the deck about 2 feet forward of the rudder. The cables should bend as little as possible, therefore the points where the cables are attached to the rudder,

do, consider how much effort you've already put into the project.

You must apply some type of finish to your boat. A couple of coats of epoxy may look like varnish, but epoxy deteriorates in sunlight, turning milky and dull. The kayak needs to be protected with either paint or varnish. Most paddlers want to finish their hull, deck, and interior bright. (You'll also need to varnish inside your kayak; sunlight strikes there, too.)

Epoxy saturation fills the wood's grain that's been opened by bending. A foam roller applies a smooth, even coat.

However, there's an argument to be made for painting the hull. Paint holds up better than varnish, is more abrasion resistant, is easier to touch up, and does not require as many coats. In addition, you can use fairing compound to achieve a smoother, more efficient, and faster hull. Even large scratches or chips in the wood can be repaired with fairing compound and hidden under paint. But, surprisingly, surface irregularities and poor sanding seem more visible on a painted surface than a varnished one. I think this is because people are a little awestruck by shiny expanses of varnished wood, and they don't notice the surface details under the varnish. One last point: you can always paint over the varnish later, but there isn't much hope of varnishing over the paint.

Epoxy Saturation

Prior to varnishing or painting your kayak, saturate its hull with unthickened epoxy. The epoxy soaks into the wood, filling and reinforcing the wood's grain, particularly the grain opened by bending. Saturation adds a tough outer skin that increases the hull's abrasion resistance and strength. In addition, epoxy provides a smooth, clear base that adds depth to the final finish.

If I'm building a kayak that's to be infrequently used, I only epoxy saturate the hull, but if it's to be used in the ocean or for long trips, I'll apply epoxy to the deck as well. If you decide not to epoxy the deck, give it its initial coat of varnish now.

As mentioned earlier, epoxy doesn't flow or level well, so applying a smooth coat is difficult. Again, the best tool for applying epoxy is a foam roller. Roll a thin layer of epoxy over the entire surface; most of this first coat will be absorbed into the wood. Rollers tend to leave small bubbles on the epoxy's surface. These must be tipped-off by running a disposable foam or bristle brush over the fresh epoxy; just skim the surface with the brush's tip to pop the bubbles. Brush out any runs or drips, or you will have to sand them out later. When the epoxy has started to cure, roll on the second coat and, again, brush out any bubbles and runs. Be particularly careful to seal exposed plywood edges, such as the underside of the coaming; if water enters the plywood's core, it can cause problems later.

Sheathing the Hull with Fiberglass

Many kayak builders routinely apply a layer of fiberglass to the kayak's hull for increased abrasion resistance, stiffness, and strength. If the kayak will be dragged across the beach or paddled in an area

Any bubbles can be popped by tipping off the epoxy with a disposable brush. Run the brush very lightly over the entire surface.

with a rocky shoreline, sheathing with fiberglass is a good idea; if you're really tough on your boat, Kevlar cloth can be substituted for fiberglass.

But if you make a habit of getting out of your boat in ankle-deep water and not dragging it up the beach, you don't need a fiberglass-covered bottom. Not glassing the hull will save you a day's work and 4 to 6 pounds of weight. You've already applied two strips of heavy fiberglass tape to the exterior hull seams, so the most vulnerable areas are already protected. I don't glass my kayaks, and they seem to hold up very well; of course, I'm more careful with them than I might be if the hulls were glassed.

If you decide to fiberglass your hull, you'll need a length of 4- or 6-ounce fiberglass cloth as long as the boat. Start by turning the hull upside down and wiping it with acetone to remove any dust or chemical contamination. Stretch the fiberglass cloth over the hull and run your hands along it to smooth out the wrinkles. At the bow and stern, cut long darts in the cloth, so its shape approximates that of the hull panels.

Use staples, push pins, or masking tape to secure the cloth to the gunnel and keel line. Let the excess cloth just hang below the boat. Rather than brushing on the epoxy, pour it along the keel line and work it into the cloth with a squeegee. Completely saturate the cloth as you did the tape. Work fast—you have a large area to cover. When the epoxy coat has started to cure, trim off the excess cloth hanging below the hull. Apply two or more additional resin coats to fill the cloth's weave.

Sanding and Fairing

No matter how carefully you rolled, brushed, or squeegeed the epoxy resin onto your hull and deck, it will not be perfectly smooth. And even if the surface was perfect, varnish or paint won't adhere properly to unsanded epoxy. You'll need to spend at least a few hours sanding and fairing.

Before you start sanding, wash the boat with detergent and water to remove the surface film that curing epoxy leaves; detergent that contains ammonia works best. This waxy film, called *amine blush*, clogs sandpaper and prevents paint and varnish from drying. Two thorough washes with a sponge and warm, soapy water followed by a rinse should remove it.

Use 80-grit paper on your sander, or 120-grit if sanding by hand. Most of the sanding will be concentrated at the seams; the major part

Sanding is best done outside. Wear a mask: who knows what epoxy dust will do to your brain?

of the hull should be almost smooth, except for runs in the epoxy. Sand the entire hull, giving the most attention to the seams and the edges of the tape. When you've finished, there should be no shiny spots remaining to indicate a low or unsanded area. If you accidently sand through the epoxy layer—and you probably will—recoat the area and sand it later.

Some builders like to roll on several more coats of epoxy after the initial sanding. This builds up a deep glasslike base for the varnish. Of course, they have to sand the subsequent coats. I've done this on one kayak, and the finish is very impressive—but it sure was a lot of work.

After sanding, you'll need to wash the kayak again to remove the sanding dust. Epoxy dust is tenacious stuff that won't just rinse off with a casual spray. You need to go over the boat several times with a wet towel or sponge.

If the hull is to be painted, use fairing compound to fill any low spots or surface pinholes. The compound is a fast-setting, easily sanded, two-part epoxy or polyester putty. It's available at any marine store. Because it's not clear, fairing compound can't be used under varnish. But you can brush on extra epoxy resin to fill low spots under varnish.

Apply the fairing compound with a putty knife or the applicators available from auto-parts stores that are used for bodywork. (They work as well as the much more expensive brands sold at marine stores.) Mix the fairing compound on translucent-plastic pallets sold for this purpose, or on pieces of stiff cardboard. But prior to mixing the fairing compound, circle all the spots that need filling with a pencil. When this is done, apply the mixture to any area that seems low; spread it with the applicator as if spackling a wall, and pay particular attention to the edges of taped seams. Some fairing compounds set up within a few minutes, therefore be prepared to work fast.

Sand the compound with your finishing sander, then with 120-grit paper on a rubber sanding block. Normally, I'll circle a kayak half a dozen times, repeatedly marking low spots, spreading fairing compound, and sanding it. If you learn not to apply more compound than is necessary to fill a depression, it only takes about 15 minutes, to spread and sand the stuff; this doesn't include curing time. If you're after a truly professional paint job, wet sand the entire hull with 220-grit paper after fairing.

Choosing a Varnish

Use only high-quality marine varnish on your kayak. Marine varnishes have ultraviolet filters that allow them to resist the deteriorating effects of sunlight longer than other varnishes. Stick to established marine brands such as Z-Spar, Epifanes, Interlux, and Woolsey. Varnishing isn't easy; don't make it tougher by using an inferior household varnish.

Each of the above-mentioned manufacturers makes several types of varnish. There are subtle differences between all the types as well as the brands. Much of varnishing involves getting a feel for the varnish you're using, so don't change brands or types once you've got the hang of it. I use Z-Spar's Captain's Varnish for 90 percent of my work. If I'm feeling bold, I might use Z-Spar's Flagship varnish on the final coats, since it builds a little thicker. However, I'd never use it as a first coat because it doesn't dry well over epoxy. See what I mean about learning to use one type?

Two-part polyurethane varnishes have recently become popular. They dry very hard, are abrasion resistant, resist sunlight well, and are compatible with epoxy. Despite these advantages, many builders still prefer traditional oil-based varnishes. I've tried two-part polyurethanes, but I'm still undecided about them because they're very expensive, harder to apply than oil-based varnish, and relatively untested. This type of varnish is essentially a clear paint, so if you use it, follow the instructions for applying two-part polyurethane paint.

Choosing Paint

Two-part polyurethane should probably be called three-part polyurethane because it must be thinned with a special solvent. It's best applied with a foam roller and tipped out with a foam brush.

Of the types of paint I've tried, the three I'll cover here are the most satisfactory. One of these should suit most builders; they include latex house paint, marine enamel, and two-part polyurethane.

Though you may snicker, latex house paint is actually not a bad choice; it is cheap, readily available in almost any color, and easy to apply. Of course, it's not too glossy or abrasion resistant, but if applied carefully and allowed to dry for a week or so before the boat is used, you'd be surprised. I've had boatshop pundits ask if it was marine enamel or polyurethane I'd used on my latex-coated boat. Despite the instructions on the can, latex paint seems to take weeks to truly dry; you can use your boat after 48 hours, but try not to scrape the still-soft paint. If you want a quick-and-dirty paint job, try latex; at least you can clean your tools and brushes in water.

Marine enamels are the traditional oil-based paints. They give a hard, reasonably glossy, abrasion-resistant finish. They are not expensive, as marine paints go, and are available in many colors. On the down side, some marine enamels don't dry well over epoxy. Many builders prefer the one-part polyurethanes to traditional enamels because they are harder and glossier.

I've started using two-part, or linear, polyurethane. It's much harder and glossier than any other paint I've used. In fact, I'm told that manufacturers have painted their fiberglass show boats with it because it's glossier than gelcoat. Unfortunately, two-part polyurethane is more expensive and harder to apply than most other paints. The extreme gloss and relative thinness of this paint brings out every flaw in the underlying surface, so you must prepare your hull with fanatical care before applying it.

There are numerous other paints on the market, and new ones are being introduced constantly. Most marine paint companies have technical representatives that will happily discuss the merits and application of their products with you. But not all paints are compatible with epoxy resin, so if you're using a new paint, first coat a small area as a test.

In choosing the color of your paint, consider whether you'll be able to get more of it when you need to touch up a scrape. White paint is always available; "minty teal" will (hopefully) be discontinued soon. Actually, there are several reasons to choose a white hull: kayaks painted a light color are cooler in the sun; many paddlers think that light-colored hulls look better with a varnished deck; scratches don't show up as easily on a white hull; and white is visible from a distance.

Tools for Finishing

The top professional yacht painters and varnishers I've met apply finishes either with a cheap, disposable foam brush and roller or with a top-quality, very expensive, badger bristle brush; they don't use anything in between. So I've switched to using disposable foam brushes and rollers; not only are they cheaper, but you don't have to clean them. I still keep a badger bristle brush around for little touch-up jobs. If you object to using disposable brushes for environmental reasons, think about how much brush cleaner you'd use to clean a bristle brush in the course of painting your kayak. The large, relatively flat surfaces of a kayak are difficult to coat with a brush; therefore, consider using a foam roller. It's a little tricky using a roller with varnish, but once you get the hang of it, it's very fast and effective.

Paint and varnish can also be applied with a spray gun, but it requires special skills that most of us don't have. If you decide to spray, contact the manufacturer for specific instructions. Some marine paints are incredibly toxic and a positive-pressure respirator must be worn while spraying.

You may have noticed a paint stripe covering the hull-to-deck joint on some kayaks; these are very difficult to paint without using masking tape. Use the plastic 3M "fine-line" tape, not regular paper masking tape. The trick to getting a nice clean line is to press the edge

Use masking tape to prevent varnish from seeping onto your paint.

down firmly, so paint can't seep under it. Don't leave masking tape in place for more than a couple of days, or it may take two more days to remove it.

Applying Varnish and Paint

The first thing you should do prior to painting or varnishing is to read the directions on the can. No one knows more about that type of paint or varnish than its manufacturer, and the advice is right there in front of you. Most manufacturers also give out free literature full of tips on applying their products; Interlux even includes a how-to audiotape with one of their paints. Most of the instructions are devoted primarily to preparing the surface prior to painting—I know you've probably heard this before, but it's important enough to repeat: preparation really is 90 percent of a good finish job.

Varnish and paint are very sensitive to temperature and humidity. If possible, varnish or paint only on warm dry days. If you're working outdoors, put the finish on early so it's almost dry before the dew starts to form in the evening. Avoid painting or varnishing outdoors on very hot days, cold days, windy days, or when there are lots of bugs around. Lastly, if there's any chance it might rain, don't varnish outdoors; if it's already raining don't even varnish indoors.

Whether you're painting or varnishing, sand lightly between coats. If applying a two-part polyurethane, wet-sand before the final coat.

It may sound as if there are only a couple of days a year when you can paint or varnish, but here are a couple of tricks you can use to expand the finishing "window." On cool days, below 60 degrees, add a little Japan drier to your varnish or oil-based paint to make it dry faster. On hot days, above 80 degrees, thin your varnish or paint with a little turpentine or marine penetrol to make it brush easier. These tricks don't work with polyurethanes, so follow the manufacturer's directions.

There's nothing like a few coats of varnish to bring out the beauty of your wooden deck.

Prior to painting or varnishing, wash your boat again to remove the amine blush that has formed while you were sanding as well as remaining traces of sanding dust. Consider wetting the floor of your shop so you won't kick up any dust while working. Finally, wipe down the boat with a tack cloth. Two-part polyurethane is very sensitive to impurities, so if you'll be using it also wipe down the hull with solvent-wash.

Never use varnish or paint directly out of the can; instead, pour as much as you'll need for one coat into a clean cup or can. And when you finish, don't think of pouring the remainder back into the can. If you'll be using a foam roller, pour the paint or varnish into a clean roller tray.

Don't overload a roller with paint or varnish. Try to apply thin even coats over the entire surface. Work quickly so you're always rolling into a wet edge rather than into paint or varnish that has started to set. Have an assistant tip off the finish by lightly running a foam brush over it to pop the bubbles and smooth out the coat. If you're working alone, you'll need to hurry to tip off the finish yourself. It's common to get a surface finish that looks stippled, or like an orange peel, when using a roller. I believe this is caused by trying to apply too thin a coat or by a dusty surface.

If you are using a brush, put on a thin coat with long, quick brush strokes, working each stroke into the coating you just put down. Keep looking back for spots you missed or runs starting to form. These

Run the elastic cord through plastic or metal eyelets (available at marine stores) or through loops of nylon strap that are screwed to the sheer clamps. If you use nylon loops, add a finish washer over the nylon to prevent the loop from pulling off the screw head. I normally use ¼-inch elastic cord for deck tie-downs; it's a little thicker than you'll see on some kayaks, but the cord holds the gear more securely and only costs a few cents more.

Compasses, Bilge Pumps, and Other Deck-mounted Gear

One of the great things about having a wooden boat is that it's easy to modify. Compasses, bilge pumps, fishing-rod holders, water-bottle holders, or most anything else you think of can be mounted on deck. In most cases, all you need to do is glue a backing plate under the deck and screw your new toy to it.

If you decide to install a compass, consider mounting it on the forward-hatch cover. This position has a couple of advantages: the compass is far enough forward that you see it over gear stowed under the tie-downs, and is easier on your eyes than trying to read a compass that's too close to the cockpit. To make sure that nothing happens to the compass, the forward hatch can be replaced with a plain hatch when you transport the boat or leave it unattended on your roof rack.

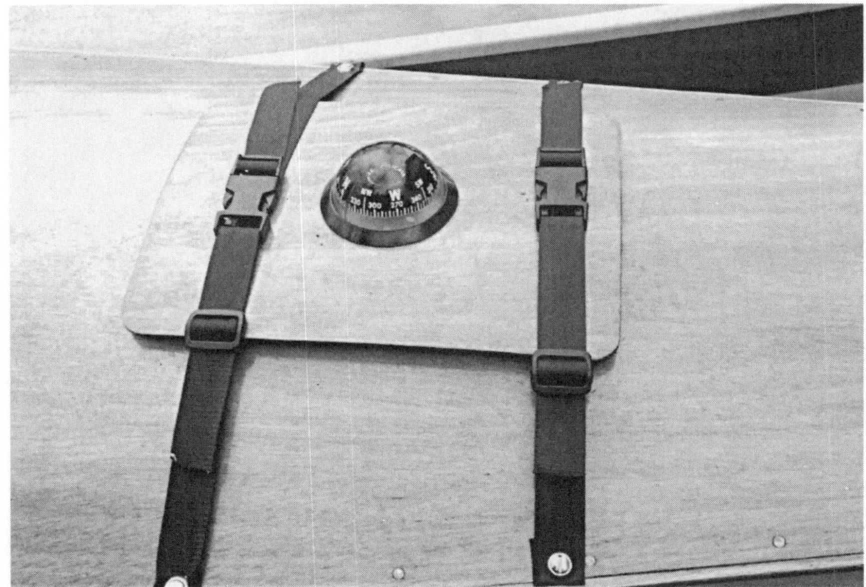

This compass is mounted on the forward hatch. The hatch and compass can be replaced with a plain hatch when the kayak is left on a car rack.

Bilge pumps are another vital safety feature on sea kayaks. You can carry a hand-held pump in the cockpit, under the deck tie-downs or you can install a diaphragm-type pump on deck. If you decide for a deck-mounted pump, position it near the aft-deck beam and glue a generously sized backing plate under the deck. The plate is needed because you can exert substantial pressure on the deck when operating a diaphragm-type pump.

Cockpit Padding

A comfortable cockpit is essential to a pleasant paddling experience. I am convinced that almost any cockpit can be made comfortable with the addition of closed-cell foam padding. Closed-cell foam also provides extra flotation, and, since it doesn't absorb water, it can be wiped dry before you get in your boat.

Half-inch foam is available from kayak shops, outdoor stores, and camping stores (where it's sold as pads for sleeping bags). Glue the foam into place with contact cement. The cement is quick and easy to use and not very strong. If you don't use too much of it, you can rip

Closed-cell foam of the type used for sleeping bag pads is perfect for padding cockpits.

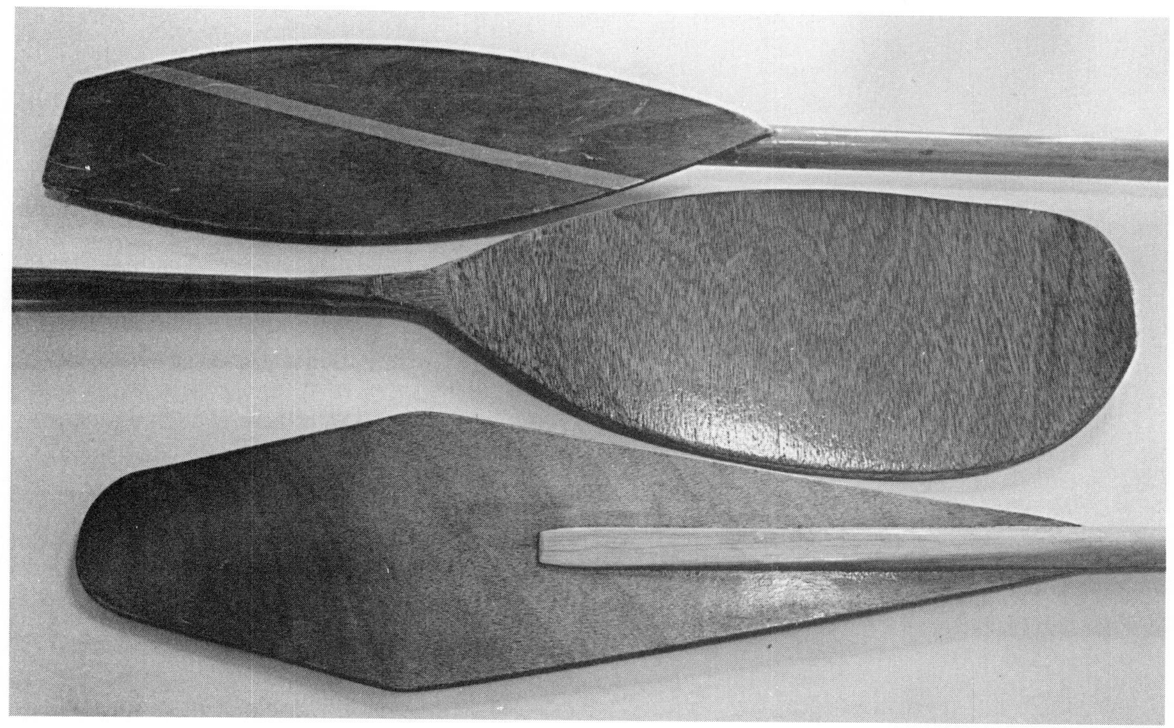

These paddles are easy to make, light, and pleasant to use.

the foam out and replace it when it starts to get flat. Pad your back-rest, seat, and the area under the deck where you brace your knees. But remember that raising the height of your seat adversely affects the kayak's stability.

Paddles

When choosing a type and length of paddle, it's wise to try out as many different types as possible. Generally, narrow-bladed paddles and paddles with small blade areas are less tiring to use on long trips and in windy conditions. An advantage to paddles with larger blade areas and modern asymmetrical designs is that they allow more control and higher speeds. Shorter paddles and smaller blade areas result in a higher stroke rate than larger-blade-area paddles. Feathered paddles, that is paddles with the blades set at right angles to each other, are more efficient in head winds, but they can cause wrist problems.

The length of your paddle will be influenced by your build and paddling style, but here are some starting points. For narrower boats, such as the Yare, a 7-foot 6-inch-long paddle is about right; for wider kayaks, like the Pocomoke, a paddle about 8 feet long is best.

Kayak paddles are expensive, and well-made wooden paddles can be difficult to find. Fortunately, you can build a serviceable kayak paddle in about six hours. These paddles are made by gluing plywood blades onto solid-wood shafts. With a little whittling and planing, they can be made very light, attractive, and efficient. I admit that I usually use a "store-bought" paddle, but I've made several spare paddles for friends who want to borrow one of my kayaks. I've also made two very long paddles for my Klepper double kayak.

The blades for these paddles are made from ¼-inch or 4mm marine plywood. Rather than use regular ¼-inch plywood I prefer to laminate two layers of 3mm plywood—some is always left over from kayak hulls or decks. This method produces a stiffer blade with more laminations. The paddles' shafts are made from 1¼-inch fir closet poles. You might need to look through a whole pile of poles to find one suitable for a paddle shaft. Look for a pole that's light; straight; has tight, straight grain; and has no knots. You can also carve the shaft from a solid spruce 2 x 2. Another type of shaft can be made by laminating two pieces of 1-inch half-round molding to a 1- x ¼-inch spacer. The ¼-inch-thick blade slides between the moldings and up to the spacer.

I've also seen homemade paddles carved from solid boards, but I don't care for them; they aren't easy to make, and they are often too narrow and heavy. The best wooden paddles are carved from laminated solid-wood strips; they are my favorite type of paddle, so I'll happily pay an expert to make them for me.

The only special tool you might need to make paddles is a spokeshave. A spokeshave allows you to quickly and easily shape the scooped-out area onto which the blade is glued. If you're buying a spokeshave, spend a bit more for the type with knobs that adjust the blade's depth. You can also carve out the scoop with a rasp, draw knife, belt sander, or, if you're a skilled carver, your pocket knife.

Plans for Two Paddles

These plans were originally drawn as full-size patterns, so the builder could simply trace the shape onto the blade blank. Because they couldn't be reproduced here at full size, I've added some dimensions that you can use to make full-size drawings. Or you could take this book to a large-copy shop and have the plans reproduced at full size. (Don't try this with kayak plans; there will be far too much distortion.)

The sleek and speedy Patuxent 17.5 has a slightly upswept bow.

This is a Cape Charles for kids. It's built exactly like the original and it's awfully cute.

Patuxent 17.5

LOA: 17½ feet
Beam: 22 inches
Weight: 36 pounds

This narrow hard-chine kayak is built much like the Cape Charles but is faster, lower, tippier, and more fun to paddle. It's designed for the skilled paddler who wants a high-performance Greenland-style kayak but needs to be able to carry enough gear for a week-long trip. I consider this my best-looking design to date.

Severn

LOA: 14½ feet
Beam: 26 inches
Weight: 28 pounds

Pictured on page 21, this compounded plywood design is a stable day-touring kayak. Its efficient hull (low wetted surface area) shape allows weaker, or less skilled, paddlers to keep up at normal touring speeds. Though some builders do paddle their Severns on the ocean, it was designed as a flatwater boat.

The Tred Avon double is built just like a big Cape Charles.

Tred Avon

LOA: 21 feet
Beam: 29 inches
Weight: 60 pounds

The Tred Avon is a roomy coastal-touring double based on the Cape Charles design. It can be built out of four 4 × 8 sheets of 4mm plywood in either an open- or a two-cockpit configuration.

Index

S

T